Tropical
Gardens

The Deutsche Nationalbibliothek lists this publication in the Deutsche Nationalbibliographie; detailed bibliographical data are available on the internet at http://dnb.ddb.de

ISBN 978-3-03768-143-5
© 2013 by Braun Publishing AG
www.braun-publishing.ch

1st edition 2013

Project coordination: Manuela Roth, Editorial Office van Uffelen
Art direction: Michaela Prinz, Berlin
Layout: Manuela Roth, Lisa Rogers

Manuela Roth

Tropical Gardens

Hidden Exotic Paradises

BRAUN

Contents

Preface

by Chris van Uffelen

Tropical gardens are little pieces of paradise on earth; bringing everything associated with paradise together in one place: a shady place to relax, to listen to the gentle splash of water, to watch as a soft breeze plays with the palm leaves above, and where ripe fruit can be enjoyed directly from the comfort of a sunbed. Here, your soul can take flight in a garden that embodies relaxation and well-being.

This volume shows handpicked examples of places where all worries melt away into the luxurious greenery. Extravagant plants grow in abundance in the sun-drenched humid climate of the equator regions. The word 'tropics' itself comes from a translation of the Greek name Trópoi Hĕliou. The Central and North parts of South America, Central Africa, South-East Asia and North Australia all lie between the lines of latitude 23° 27' North and South on both sides of the equator. Here, it is difficult to distinguish between the different seasons – with an alluring annual average of 25° Celsius, both day and night.

Of course, this magnificent lush greenery doesn't just require sunlight, but also water; otherwise it would quickly become savannah or even desert. The tropics have the highest levels of rainfall in the world and vegetation grows accordingly. Some plants, when grown outside of the tropics, require careful attention and expertise to encourage them to grow at all, here these same plants grow like weeds on the sidewalk.

The tropics offer a huge variety of vegetation. The tropical dry forests host succulents and teak wood, while the rainforests provide the perfect environment for bromeliads, orchids and rubber trees. The tropics also have their own scent. Not just the smell of damp flora, but also of bananas, ginger, figs, vanilla, coffee, cocoa and cinnamon – useful plants that grow here in abundance and characterize our own idea of a tropical paradise. One also hears birds, such as macaws, toucans, and hummingbirds, or a monkey on a branch, frogs in a pond or sunning themselves on a stone, or one sees a gecko moving soundlessly through the undergrowth. Visitors to these gardens though have more in common with the sloths who live here: just enjoying hanging out in nature or lazily gliding through the water.

Water features are also a typical component of a tropical garden, serving not just leisure activities but also climatization. Pools, streams and small waterfalls open out the space and structure it, serving as a tempting attraction in a sea of voluptuous green foliage. Pavilions and terraces also help to vary the space, often deliberately overgrown, veiled with green or covered by dry palm leaves. It is here that visitors can meet and enjoy the ambience, watch the Buddha figures that peek out from between the leaves, or enjoy fresh tea and fruit. These spaces are often strongly geometric – creating a delightful contrast to the sweeping lines of the surrounding nature, and also often incorporating it in terms of the material used or by mimicking the contrast of light and shadow cast by dense foliage. Garden furnishings often play with similarities and differences. Strong forms and pure colors separate the small tables, sofas and chairs from the garden. Deliberately chosen materials become a tactile experience, while natural surfaces seek to re-establish a connection to nature. Every reader will find his or her own personal idea of paradise tucked within the pages of this volume, a place that speaks to both the body and soul.

from above to below: pavilion raised above pond, patio and fountain surrounded by lush foliage

pavilions and connecting bridges raised above water on stilts

Howie's House

Mae Rim, Thailand

Landscape architect: Bill Bensley
Architect: Bill Bensley
Year of completion: 2005
Gross floor area: 11,750 m²
Design elements: water gardens, statues, ornaments
Plants: Areca catechu, Copernicia prunifera, Cyrtostachys renda, Steritzia nicolai, Schizostachyum brachycladum, Dracaena loureiri, Bromeliads, heliconias, Etlingera elatior, Cyperus papyrus

Designed by Bensley Architects, this property is adjacent to the Four Seasons Resort Chiang Mai and comprises seven main structures, which include living and dining areas, bedroom suites, studios and private quest pavilions – as well as three additional salas. The pavilions are hidden discreetly amongst the four acres of vibrant tropical gardens, peaceful streams and majestic water gardens.

The garden encourages visitors to explore the lush landscape and to loose themselves amongst the tranquil pools and vibrant plants. The design includes approximately 20 different sub-gardens, each with its own character. The designers purchased carefully selected plants to create this unique garden.

9

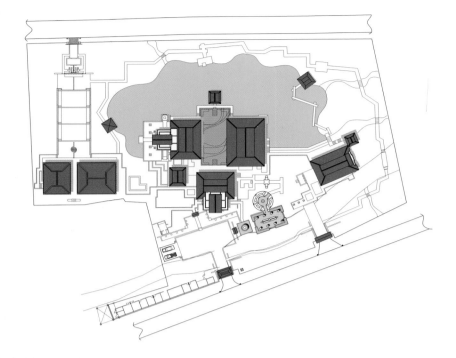

from left to right, above to below: site plan, detail, pagoda, ornamental elements surrounded by trees and foliage

from left to right, above to below: patio with elephant statues,
statues hidden in foliage, path wanders through garden

11

from left to right, above to below: bridge half hidden by creeping plants, bridge and water feature, traditional architectural design complements landscaping

from left to right, above to below: terrace juts out over water, rustic furniture complements architectural style, raised walkways, relaxing seating area surrounded by water

from left to right, above to below: atmospheric sanctuary, relaxing place to sit and enjoy the scenery, decorative detail

pavilion architecture in tranquil setting

Baan Botanica

Bangkok, Thailand

Landscape architect: Bensley Design Studios
Architect: Bill Bensley
Year of completion: 2011
Gross floor area: 500 m²
Design elements: wood, pocket gardens, pool
Plants: about 120 species of tropical plants including heliconias, palms, philodendrons

Tucked into a small soi (lane) in Bangkok's outer suburbs, and fortified by laterite walls and a bell tower, this home is a quiet green sanctuary. Baan Botanica's garden is an intimate series of pocket gardens; all unique, and peppered with unusual tropical plants and ornaments. One garden leads to the next through a series of gates, the bell tower and a massage pavilion. The garden includes three outdoor-indoor dining areas: the newest is a free-standing pavilion in the garden that incorporates four sets of antique wooden doors from the northern Thai province of Sukhothai. The second area is a reclaimed wooden table positioned alongside the pool. The third is on the verandah, which wraps around three sides of this Thai colonial-style home, and overlooks the lawn and pool.

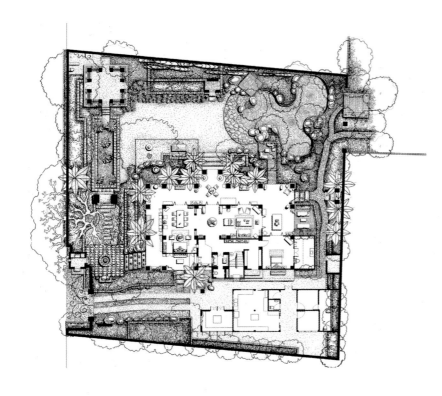

from left to right, above to below: house and garden plan, interior meets exterior, garden decorated with extraordinary ornaments, garden is an intimate arrangement of pocket gardens

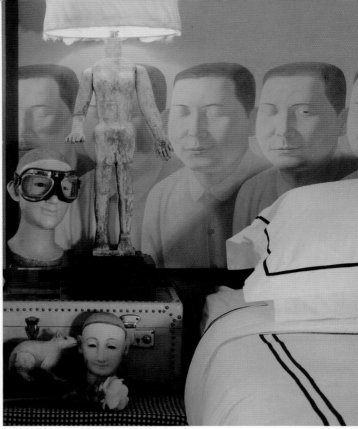

from left to right, above to below: hidden seating area, bedroom,
design blurs the boundaries between interior and exterior space

beautiful contrast of colors and textures

from left to right, above to below: water garden, interior design complements garden, open seating area on the lawn

from above to below: lush foliage encroaches onto terrace, land-scaped pool

from left to right, above to below: foliage surrounds house and overhangs terrace, planting detail, house surrounded by lawn and trees

Prime Nature Residence

Bangkok, Thailand

Landscape architect: Pichai Jiropas
Architect: Department of Architecture Co.
Year of completion: 2011
Gross floor area: 480 m²
Design elements: metal lattice screens, canvas panels
Plants: Royal palm, Burma padauk, Dolichandrone spathacea schum, cork, Antidesma velutinosum blume, Ivory Coast almond, bamboo

The owner's brief for this residence seems rather simple at first – his bedroom on ground floor, another bedroom on the second floor, a large interior living space, and an outdoor terrace and garden. However, the location presented an interesting challenge, situated at a busy intersection in an upscale residential estate that forbids the use of any kind of fences. Metal lattice screens and sheer canvas panels dominate the architecture. At night,

periphery trees catch trespassing car headlights and cast their shadows on deliberately placed canvas planes. Trees surround the garden, giving it some much-needed privacy, and the lush greenery continues all the way up to the terrace, where it encroaches over the railing, creating a tranquil place to relax that really feels as if it is part of the garden.

from above to below: terrace offers a tranquil place to relax,
architecture merges interior and exterior

from above to below: house at night, house and site plan

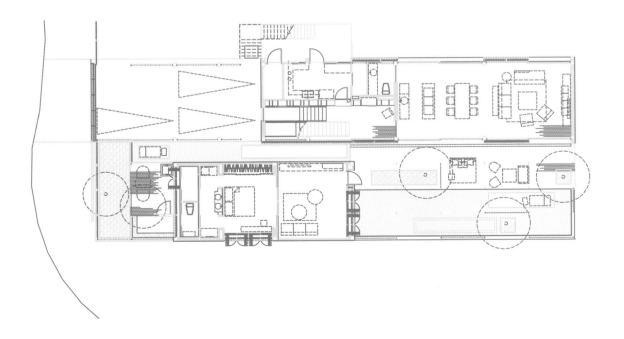

from above to below: pathway winds across the site, terracotta-
tiled house has a very open-plan design

from left to right, above to below: tiled roofed verandah that envelopes the central courtyard, vernacular architecture blurs boundaries between inside and outside, lily pool

Bellad House

Karnataka, India

Landscape architect: Dewa Kusuma – NC Design & Associates, Khosla Architects
Architect: Khosla Architects
Year of completion: 2011
Gross floor area: 11,000 m²
Design elements: central courtyard wrapped around verandah, lily and fish pools
Plants: gulmohar, frangipani, coconut trees, raphis palms and ginger lilies

This house is set on a wooded site and the architects got their inspiration for the design from an old towering Gulmohar tree and peacocks that strutted freely across the site. The house weaves itself around this natural environment. The open-plan house is a low terracotta-tiled structure with large windows and terraces that flood the interior with light. A central courtyard opens out to the sky, creating a dialogue between interior and exterior spaces. The courtyard is surrounded by a verandah, which provides a flexible space for reading, dining or just sitting and relaxing. A dining pavilion opens out to the landscaped garden. A fishpond and water lily pool is located between the two children's rooms.

from left to right, above to below: verandah and garden, entrance driveway
leads from the north-east entrance to the main portico, dining pavilion

from left to right, above to below: lily pool with Frangipani tree and blue wall in backdrop, verandah overlooking central courtyard, fish pools flanking children's bedrooms, site plan

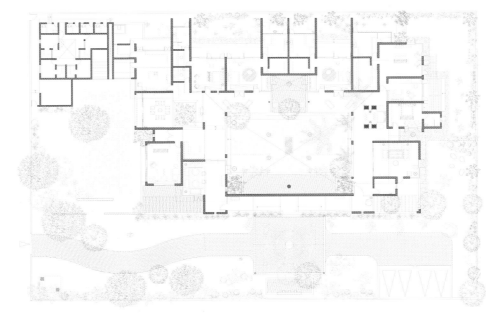

from left to right, above to below: sunken garden around the stepped well near the main house, bath garden viewed from the kid's verandah, view of the pathway to the first house through the rocks in the entrance garden

view of first house from entrance garden

South-Indian Retreat

South India

Landscape architect: Mancini Enterprises
Horticulturist: Govinda Luke Bowley
Architect: Mancini Enterprises
Year of completion: 2009
Gross floor area: 1,000 m²
Design elements: sunken garden, roof overhangs, small forest
Plants: palms, plumeria, succulents, agaves, Phyllostachys nigra, Bambusa ventricosa, local grass varieties

This 4,000-square-meter compound has been turned into an interior world consisting of three houses; pool with pavilion; small forest; rock, tropical, and suspended gardens, as well as a sunken garden around a deep well, outdoor bathrooms, savanna and water tank, all assembled to provide views of the nearby holy mountain and yet creating privacy with its different indoor and outdoor spaces. Sloping roof gardens provide natural connectivity from the living quarters on the first floors down to the common spaces on the ground floor and the visitor discovers a new space or a new vista around every corner.

The buildings draw on traditional construction techniques combined with large roof overhangs and high thermal mass thus ensuring cool interiors in the very hot climate of the south Indian countryside. All architectural and interior elements are custom designed and manufactured by local craftsmen whereas the infrastructural elements rely on technology to ensure environmental sustainability.

from left to right, above to below: view of the sunken garden located around the stepped well, main lawn from the terrace garden, guest house in the middle of the savannah garden

from left to right, above to below: view of the rock garden near the first house, roof garden adjacent to the master bedroom, view of the roof garden above and the tropical garden below, ground floor and site plan

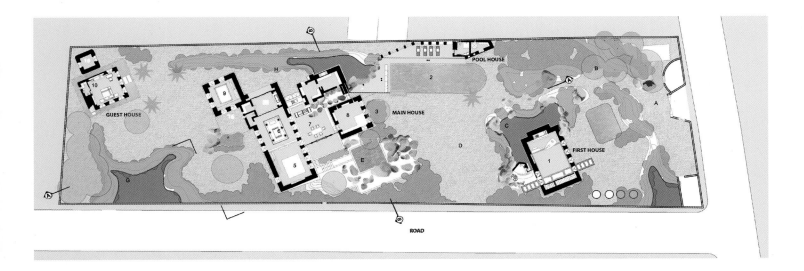

from left to right, above to below: architecture uses traditional
Balinese elements, traditional entrance, foliage

garden and architecture use steeply sloping site to great dramatic views

Villa Keliki

Bali, Indonesia

Landscape architect: Made Wijaya
Architect: Made Wijaya
Year of completion: 2005
Gross floor area: 5,400 m²
Design elements: pavilions, raised walkways,
Plants: plumerias, durian trees, tree ferns, heliconias, palms, Crinum lilies

Villa Keliki is intended as a showpiece, a stunning garden and house in a strikingly beautiful location. The project began with the grounds; once an impressive pleasure garden, the site had been let go and was badly overgrown. The tropical vegetation was trimmed back, and pathways were improved with steps of volcanic tuff, balustrades and pergolas covered with jade vines, dragon's claws and thunbergia. The architecture of the house itself reflects local traditions. The main house is a large pavilion with coconut columns, bamboo rafters and thatched roof. Other, smaller pavilions are scattered like gems across the gardens acting almost as little follies. The main pavilion, built on the site of an old garden pavilion, is accessed from the street through a pair of imposing brass gates. A hammered-copper shelter designed by Indonesian artist Pintor Sirait crowns a double staircase of river boulders leading down to the main pavilion's open-air top floor.

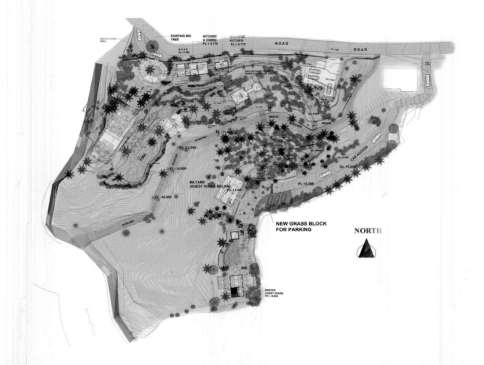

from left to right, above to below: master plan, hidden pool creates a tranquil clearing, pavilions with views of garden, bridges help to create an exciting landscape

from above to below: pavilions are a traditional part of Balinese architecture, steep terrain sculpted into a myriad of winding paths and terraces

from above to below: pavilions blend in as part of the garden, stunning views from the top of the sloping garden

from left to right, above to below: water cascades over ledge, pool fits seamlessly into landscape, hidden path, foliage gives pool privacy and shade

house offers breathtaking views of the sea

water in pool appears to flow down to the beach, blurring the boundaries between natural and manmade

Sassoon House

Uluwatu, Bali, Indonesia

Landscape architect: Made Wijaya
Architect: Uira – Artalenta Indonesia
Year of completion: 2012
Gross floor area: 1,400 m²
Design elements: pool, terraces, artistic gates and railings
Plants: Giant milkways, pandanus, plumerias, bougainvilleas, cordylines

This house is a holiday home for a Singapore family with business interests in Indonesia. The brief was for a complete makeover of a fairly formulaic tropical-modern bungalow, giving the property more of a garden home flavour, but with an edgy and modern design. For this the architects enlisted the talents of Indonesian sculptor and industrial designer Pintor Sirait to help with the design of the new doors, artistic walls and railings. The house site covers approximately 1,000 square meters and is located within a luxurious gated community. A Singapore-based Australian interior designer was called in to do a complete overhaul of the interior and a Jakarta architect, Uira of Artalenta Indonesia re-worked the space planning and finishes.

39

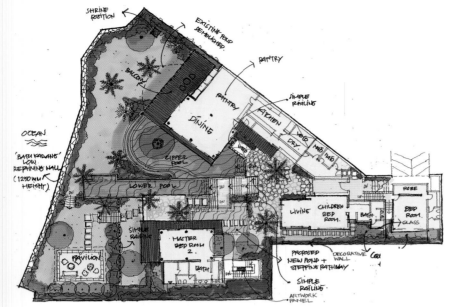

from left to right, above to below: site plan, cracked appearance of paving stones gives garden a more natural look, water garden, large windows make the most of the spectacular views

ULUWATU -

from left to right, above to below: comfortable places to relax and enjoy the scenery, terrace offers an unbeatable dining area, terrace with stunning views of the sea

from above to below: hotel villas blend in with landscape,
entrances

hotel villa cabana

Alila Villas Uluwatu

Bali, Indonesia

Landscape architect: Cicada Pte Ltd
Architect: WOHA
Year of completion: 2009
Gross floor area: 26,595 m²
Design elements: limestone rubble cladding, white sandstone, recycled Ulin timber, unpolished terrazzo, lava rocks
Plants: plumeria 'Bali yellow', Mexican lilac, sea morning glory, lemon grass, Scaevola milkweed, kapok

This hotel and villa development is a Green Globe 21 rated ecologically sustainable development. It proposes luxury as delight and enjoyment of natural beauty and sense of place, rather than excessive consumption. The design combines the delights of traditional Balinese pavilion architecture and rural landscapes with modern dynamic treatment of space and form. A terraced roof was developed using Balinese volcanic pumice rock, which is a natural insulating material. These low terraced roofs keep open the site's unique wide panoramas. The hillside villas are designed as pavilions linked by bridges across water gardens, tucked into the hillside as terraces. The local plants are adapted to the dry savannah landscape by going dormant in the dry season then flowering spectacularly and provide a unique seasonal display of flowers. These native gardens require far less water, and support local animals and birds.

from above to below: beautiful public areas, hillside villa
roofscape

from above to below: design seeks to remain as natural as possible, path leading to villas, hotel master plan

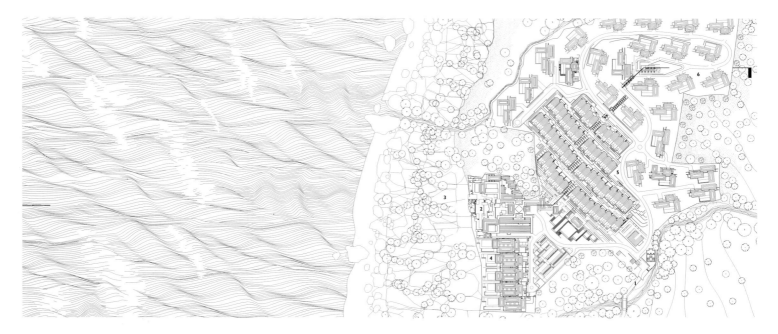

from left to right, above to below: 'common ground' or kraal surrounded by a fence, dividing wall represents a line between past and present, garden is partly wild and partly formal

dense foliage, birds of paradise and pots surround the open space
at the heart of the garden

Hortus Consensus

Nagasaki, Japan

Landscape architect: Leon Kluge Garden Designs
Year of completion: 2012
Gross floor area: 150 m²
Design elements: dividing wall, 'kraal' area, water features
Plants: Strelitzia reginae, Aloe vera, Helichrysum petiolare, Panicum 'heavy metal', Euphorbia tirucalli

Inspired by the South African experience of reconciliation and nation-building since the advent of democracy, this landscape undergoes a metamorphis that results in a mutually beneficial transformation. The dividing wall running through the garden represents the line between past and present. The natural hillside garden represents pre-existing instability and chaos, while the more formal new garden symbolizes order and consensus. The diver-

sity of color and texture found in the garden represents a productive, multi-cultural society. The focal point of the garden is a homestead or kraal – a traditional African village of huts typically enclosed by a fence. The common ground at the heart of this space is designed as a place where matters are discussed and decisions can be made. Water symbolizes life and new beginnings, falling from the crest of the hill and into the new garden as life giving rain.

from left to right, above to below: concept plan, fence separates central space, wall widens to form a bench, birds of paradise grow in decorated pot

The CoNcept 3D

seating area wrapped around communal space

from above to below: luxury and nature combine, pool extends to the infinity of the sea giving a feeling of paradise

a flawless pool for a cooling swim during long hot summer days

A Coastal Retreat

Rmeileh, Lebanon

Landscape architect: Francis Landscapes
Architect: Charles Hadife
Year of completion: 2007
Gross floor area: 20,000 m²
Design elements: pool, huts, bamboo, pool bar, cycle path
Plants: cactus, bougainvilea, palm trees, blue jasmine, banana trees, bamboo, yucca palm

Extending along a kilometer of the Lebanese southern coastline, this exclusive beach resort is nestled among exotic guava groves and is designed to open up on an untamed but tranquil sea and a magnificent setting sun. Gently slanting towards the ocean, winding pathways invite visitors to a contemplative walk or a refreshing swim in the sea. With its paradisiacal beach, lush greenery and exotic fruiting trees this project was exotic from the start. To cre-

ate a true natural haven and complete the existing Eden-esque atmosphere, raw materials, such as Ylang Ylang, were shipped in from Bali. The true jewels of this project however, are the personal serviced bungalows, with private Jacuzzis overlooking the sea and bubbling from a tailored garden that inspires comfort and escape. The architects have created a space that whisks visitors away to a destination far from the hustle and bustle of Beirut.

from left to right, above to below: sketch of resort, garden designed specifically to inspire comfort and escape, rustic architectural charm

from above to below: sun setting over the sea, beach shelters
offer shade against the tropical sun

from left to right, above to below: pool, sea and sky merge, a
natural haven, exotic huts decorated with cactus and bamboo

from left to right, above to below: exotic flowering trees and shrubs, winding pathways, greenery and exotic fruiting trees surround pool, tranquil pool landscape

from above to below: pool assumes aesthetic preeminence, pool structure frames the stunning view

tranquil pond nestles in lush greenery

This is not a Framed Garden

Bsalim, Lebanon

Landscape architect: Frederic Francis
Architect: Pierre Khoury Architects
Year of completion: 2011
Gross floor area: 6,000 m²
Design elements: porticos, pool, lily pond, gazebo, bridge, water feature
Plants: pine trees, olive trees, oak trees, bamboos, birds of paradise, laurel trees

Built on a hill with an awe-inspiring 260-degree view of Beirut and the Mediterranean Sea, this garden is integrated into the natural, hilly landscape. Ranging from a modern patio with infinity pool to a variety of themed gardens, this project is designed to be the perfect escape into one's own personal paradise. The infinity pool looks like a sheet of still water, creating a dialogue by reflecting the surroundings. This garden was created to be a place of contemplation and comfort, where wanderers are free to stroll through. With one step, they leave behind the structured world and enters a realm with lush natural forests, where all the senses are charmed, breathing with occasional clearings linked by sinuous, winding pathways. Within these collocated worlds, one's pleasures come out to be experienced through each of the senses.

geometric porticos define the space like a picture frame, inviting the onlooker to contemplate the garden

from above to below: views of beautiful scenery inspire the architecture, site plan

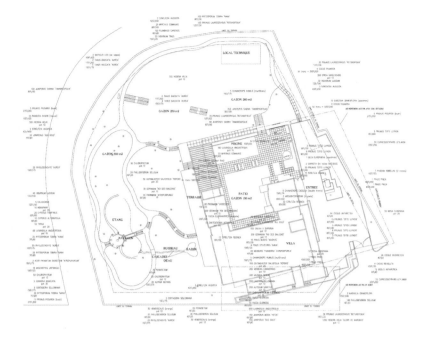

from left to right, above to below: planting plan, two imposing porticos determine the view from the pool, palm trees shade pool and garden, the pool becomes a serene vantage point from which to contemplate the striking scenery

from left to right, above to below: diverse shapes and colors complement each
other, spotlights highlight garden design, landscaping blends with nature

from left to right, above to below: tranquil Zen fountain, green spaces provide a sense of well-being, a corner that inspires comfort and escape

garden merges equilibrium and appeal

Rural Oasis

Awkar, Lebanon

Landscape architect: Frederic Francis
Architect: Pierre Khoury Architects
Year of completion: 1999
Gross floor area: 1,500 m²
Design elements: terraces, seating area, patio pool, wooden pergola
Plants: cactus, bougainvillea, palm trees, banana trees, bamboo, grenadine trees, begonias, birds of paradise

Located in a densely populated region just outside the city of Beirut, this villa and garden are actually a villa and four gardens. The mazelike garden paths create a sense of wonder in what would otherwise be a space too small for amazement. As a small city garden, it left no room for chance. Special attention was paid to the volume of the plants, the size and texture of the foliage and the color gradient, making sure everything was in perfect harmony.

The gardens radiate with an energy that cannot leave any visitor indifferent. Walking from one garden to another, the visitor goes through a succession of green spaces, where new elements appear; terraces planted with fruit bearing trees, big emerald green leaves juxtaposed with lime green shrubs and, for a meditative pause, patios, pergolas, and built in seating areas, all ideal to connect with this human-scale garden.

from left to right, above to below: an ideal spot to entertain
guests, tropical plants, entrance

from left to right, above to below: numerous species of palms and plants decorate terrace, ideal tropical outdoor, site plan

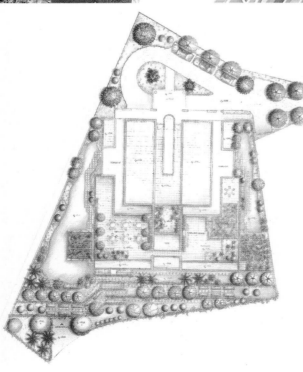

65

pool deck surrounded by lush foliage

elevated living room with views of garden terrace

Jervois Hill House

Singapore, Singapore

Landscape architect:
Dr. Easaw Thomas
Architect: AR43 Architects
Pte Ltd
Year of completion: 2009
Gross floor area: 1,076 m²
Design elements: swimming
pool, terrace
Plants: Gardenia cymmosa,
Pisonia alba, Schizolobium
parahyba, Erythrina glauca,
Dellinia indica, Areca catechu,
Coccos nucifera, and others

This house is a surprising discovery in densely populated Singapore. Located in one of the city's prime shopping districts, the house sits on a steeply sloping site studded with mature rainforest trees. Extensive landscaping using tropical plants further complements the existing landscape. Protected by large overhangs at both the east and west ends, the house is shielded from the harsh tropical sun. The house is entered via a broad flight of stairs leading to the living room – an elevated pavilion with an extensive view of the garden terrace. A linear pond wraps around one end of the pavilion, both as an injection of a natural element and also as a gesture to elaborate the linearity of the volume. A waterfall cascades down the mid level garden, plunging into the swimming pool.

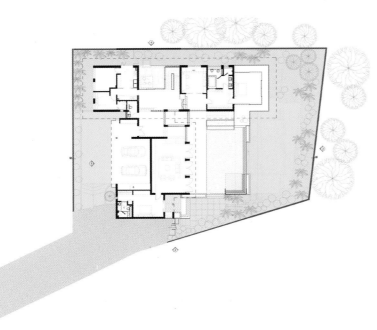

from above to below: first floor plan, pool reflects surroundings

from above to below: house surrounded by lush rainforest
trees, family room

from left to right: wide welcoming entrance, architecture merges
interior and exterior

architecture honors the landscape

Bishopsgate House

Singapore, Singapore

Landscape architect: Nyee Phoe Flower Garden
Architect: Warner Wong Design | WOW Architects
Year of completion: 2008
Gross floor area: 644 m²
Design elements: pool, terrace
Plants: Alibizia tree, Delonix Regia, Erythrinia Cristagalli, Canna Indica, Heliconia Psittacorum, Agave Angustifolia, Asplenium Nidus

Bishopsgate House was conceived and developed in harmony with its unique location, a rare heritage site in the heart of Singapore surrounded by mature trees amidst untouched swathes of secondary forest. The concept of the house evolved in celebration of the land, its curves and undulations, its birds, breezes, views, trees, soil, and bedrock. The design honors the landscape of rolling hills and giant trees and was based on stringent principles of

sustainability. From the main building, a dining pavilion protrudes into the garden with a large roof deck above overlooking the garden and pool. The quality of light in and around the house has the glow of the landscape, soft dappled shadows, and a gentle illumination. The large surface areas of the site and the roofs are employed as a strategic rainwater collector, maximizing the use of abundant rainwater.

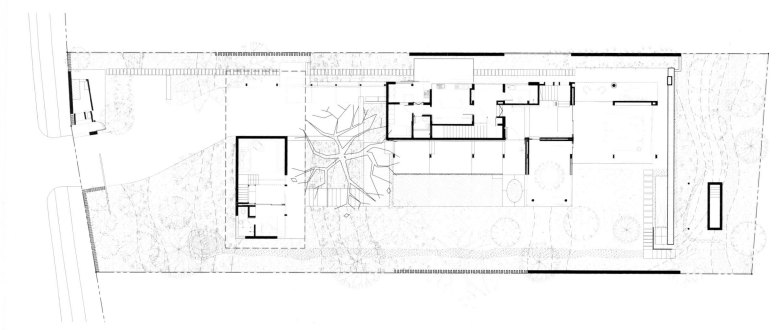

from left to right, above to below: ground floor and garden plan, lush foliage surrounds house, pool acts as an extension of the living space, house shines brightly in the evening light

from left to right, above to below: open terraces offer a peaceful place to sit, terrace protrudes into garden, tranquil pool in the midst of lush foliage

from left to right: entrance, main entrance with abundance of flowers

swimming pool and courtyard

Cluny House

Singapore, Singapore

Landscape architect:
Guz Architects
Architect: Guz Architects
Year of completion: 2006
Gross floor area: 1,165 m²
Design elements: pond for
passive cooling, green roofs
Plants: Ironwood trees,
phyllanthus, bougainvillea,
Russelia thunbergia

The Cluny House is laid out around a central water court that forms the focal point of the project. Lushly planted roof gardens surround this and add to the effect that nature is evident in every part of the house. This project also demonstrates how technology, planning and design can be applied sensitively to generate a comfortable, luxurious, yet sustainable family home. The designers' main endeavor was to create a residence with seamless integration of the surrounding nature; water played a key role in achieving that.

from above to below: entrance with overhanging roof borders pond, rooms and terraces with views of pool and garden

from left to right, above to below: garden offers many sheltered spaces to sit and relax, planted terraces give house more privacy, terrace with stunning views of garden, house and garden plan

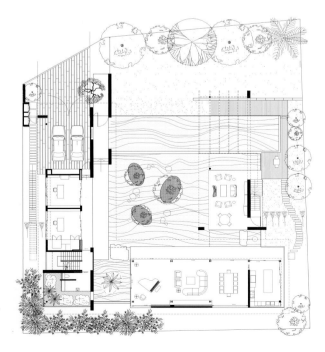

from left to right, above to below: rear of house and pool at twilight, side gar
den with lush greenery, overhanging upper story reduces house footprint

tranquil oasis surrounded by lush foliage

Sentosa House

Singapore, Singapore

Landscape architect: Tulin Designs
Architect: nicholas burns associates
Year of completion: 2012
Gross floor area: 650 m²
Design elements: reclaimed teak, off-form concrete, stone
Plants: tropical species

This house is an adaptable space, with lots of open spaces that are free from predetermined function. Materials were chosen for their inherent qualities: reclaimed golden teak, fair-faced concrete, stone and steel all offer duality of function. Their richness and texture provides the decorative element. The house is designed for the tropical climate. The reclaimed teak screen and deck fits over the concrete structure and glazing protecting it from the sun allowing the thermal mass of the concrete to stabilize the internal temperature. Cross ventilation, the other critical element of tropical design, allows even slight breezes to flow freely throughout the house. The landscape uses species that suit the climate and that thrive with minimal intervention.

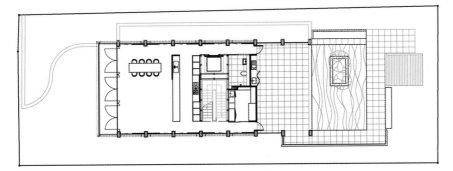

from left to right, above to below: ground floor plan, trees and foliage give house more privacy, views of landscape from master bedroom, solid stone stairs give the entrance a more natural appearance

from above to below: foliage creates a dramatic backdrop
behind pool, terrace offers a tranquil place to relax

from left to right: large windows offer views of garden, light-filled interior with views of courtyards and gardens

roof landscaping with diagonally arranged planting strips

Zig Zag House

Singapore, Singapore

Landscape architect:
Tierra Design
Architect: Ministry of Design
Year of completion: 2009
Gross floor area: 600 m²
Design elements: courtyards,
roof landscaping

Returning to the romance of a single-story bungalow, the Zig Zag House acquires its unique form via a series of formal maneuvers around a mature tree located on the long triangular site. The building's twisting form creates 'in-between' spaces, which provide shelter from nature and simultaneously allow for cross ventilation and filtered light. Tropical courtyards, permit light to flow deep into the building. The roofscape adds a final striking design touch – diagonally arranged planting strips echo the twisting form of the house.

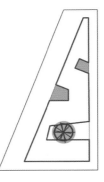  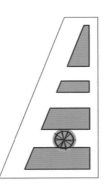 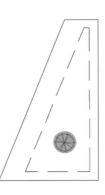 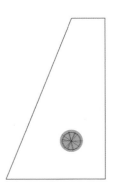

from left to right, above to below: roofscape diagrams, open-plan interior, water features offer a tranquil space to relax, garden is incorporated into the house by means of courtyards and large windows

roofscape maximizes available space

from above to below: lush tropical retreat in the middle of the
city, balcony skygarden from above

an oasis of calm amidst the city hustle and bustle

Newton Suites

Singapore, Singapore

Landscape architect: Cicada
Architect: WOHA
Year of completion: 2007
Gross floor area: 11,835 m²
Design elements: skygardens, balconies, creeper screens
Plants: plumeria, Thumbergia grandiflora, yellow iris, Boston fern

This 36-story development is a study in environmental solutions to tropical high-rise living. Protruding sky gardens and balconies, combined with sun shading screens create outdoor living environments that are sheltered and have ample cross-ventilation due to their elevated location, particularly suited to the hot tropical climate. Residential units are stacked four to each floor with habitable balconies treated as outdoor living rooms. Creeper screens are applied to otherwise blank walls to absorb sunlight and carbon and create oxygen in the dense environment. Most available horizontal and vertical surfaces are landscaped. The environmental elements added to residential apartments and extensive communal areas combine to make a unique tropical building.

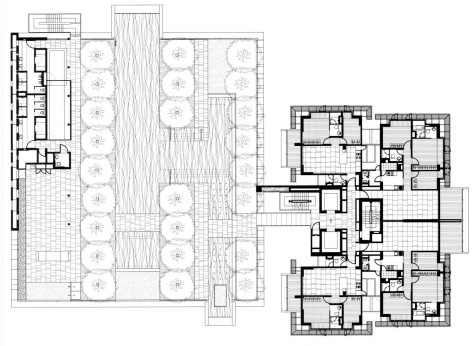

from left to right, above to below: environmental deck plan,
creeper screens decorate otherwise plain walls, view of pool from
above, façade detail

innovative tropical skygardens

from above to below: water cascades from the main pool into the Jacuzzi poo
and finally onto the step cascades fronting the lawn, bubbling Jacuzzi animat
the lower level of the pool

from left to right, above to below: view from the spiral ramp into the landscape courtyard below, central landscape area portraying an intimate secret garden, Jacuzzi at night

Duchess Residences

Singapore, Singapore

Landscape architect: Sitetectonix
Architect: MKPL Architects
Year of completion: 2011
Gross floor area: 14,400 m²
Design elements: organic and naturalistic forms expressed by a combination of stone, timber, glass, steel
Plants: 40 tree species, 70,000 shrubs and ground-covering plants

The landscape design at Duchess Residences aims to create a piece of living landscape sculpture that responds and preserves the undulating terrain of the site. It creates a lush primeval secret garden as a contemporary and exclusive setting for living. The secret garden contains three-dimensional landforms and spaces, which vary from the grand to the intimate in character. A strong intimacy with nature is pervasive in the organic forms throughout the site where planting and water interconnect. Water overflowing the long edge of the pool visibly expresses the level change in the site in a long series of cascades. The material palette used organizes the lighter beige-colored materials for use on the horizontal plane while the darker green and black stones are used in the vertical planes.

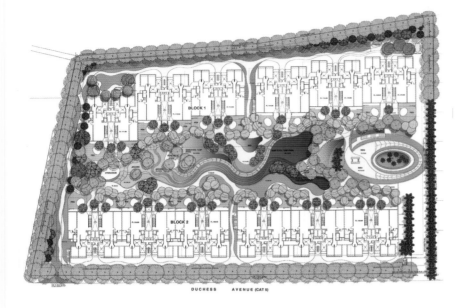

from left to right, above to below: initial design concept, aerial overview of the landscape design, canopy of the palms emerges from the void, aerial overview of the organic layering of landscape by night

from above to below: void visually connects the upper deck and lower pool, a series of
'organ pipes' act as a safety barrier and a water play feature by day

from above to below: secret path winds through undergrowth, statues hidden within dense foliage

lotus pond

Residential Garden

Brisbane, Australia

Landscape architect: Dennis Hundscheidt – Palmyra Landscaping Design
Year of completion: ongoing
Gross floor area: 3,000 m²
Design elements: garden room concept
Plants: extensive range of rare and exotic tropical plants

The original garden design dates back some 25 years and had an area of 1,000 square meters. It now comprises a total area of just over 3,000 square meters. Over one hundred species of palms, many of which were personally collected by the designer in the jungles of Indonesia and Malaysia, now form the beautiful canopy for the more colorful plantings, creating a striking color contrast. Water plays an important role in this garden and one is never far away from the gently sound of trickling water. The garden is made up of eight garden areas, linked by natural stone pathways.

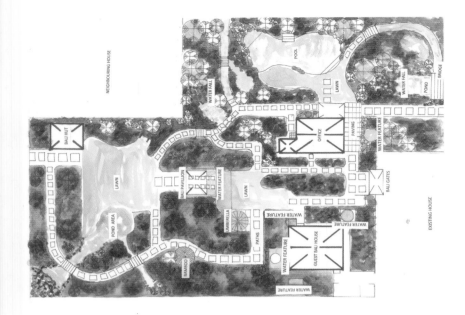

from left to right, above to below: site plan, colorful plantings create an exciting contrast, stepping stones across pond, tranquil water garden

from above to below: private seating area, pool brings to mind
a clearing in a forest

from left to right, above to below: seating area makes the most of
the views, Grevillea dryandri (pink form) and Maytown Grevillea,
lawn walk to tennis pavilion

from left to right, above to below: Heliconia acuminate, guest houses surrounded by dwarf coconut palms and red shell ginger, low stone wall with view of Mount Somerset

Mali Mali

Mialo, Australia

Landscape architect: Hortulus Landscape Design
Architect: Chris van Dyke
Year of completion: 2008
Gross floor area: 422 m²
Design elements: low stone walls, water features
Plants: Grevillea banksii, Thalia, Gardenia psidioides, Melastoma affine, Lomandra longifolia, heliconia, Hotrio nights, Heliconia rostrata, Cerbus mangus

Mali Mali sits on top of a small coastal mountain range commanding views across the Coral Sea to Low Isles in the east and to the World Heritage rainforest of the Daintree to the north and west. A long driveway sweeps up the mountain ridge from the Rainforest floor winding its way to the top. Mali Mali has a distinct feel of the Pacific Islands while being obviously grounded in the Australian Tropics. The use of Grass trees, Grevillea 'Cooroora Cascade' and Lomandra longifolia provide an unmistakable Australian feel. The pavilion style house presents its spacious rooms to the view where folding doors allow the space to be a part of the landscape. The lush planting progressively reduces and becomes distinctively tropical Australian flora as one wonders across the helipad lawn to the tennis pavilion. The property is predominantly hill top rainforest dominated with the drier gum trees.

from left to right, above to below: pool takes advantage of
hilltop site, driveway, view to the Coral Sea and Island Point
Port Douglas, water appears to cascade over pool edge

from left to right, above to below: traditional architectural style, water feature, lotus pool, site plan

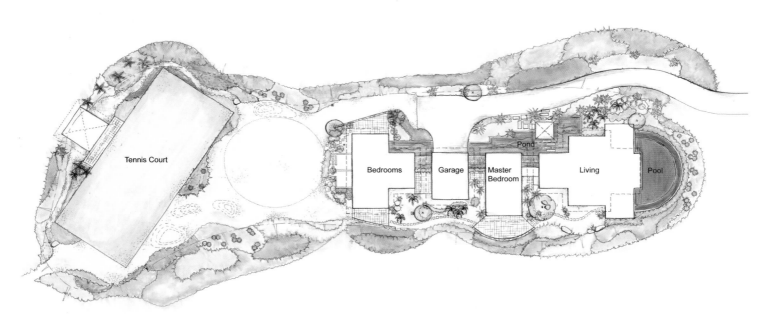

Tennis Court

Bedrooms

Garage

Master Bedroom

Pond

Living

Pool

from left to right, above to below: pool surrounded by green foliage, elegant interior opens out to garden, Heliconia lingulata

open lawn gives impression that house is in a forest clearing

Kai Hai

Port Douglas, Australia

Landscape architect: Hortulus Landscape Design
Architect: Alex Gencur
Year of completion: 2010
Gross floor area: 440 m²
Design elements: extensive use of lines, water features
Plants: Lipstick palms, Solitare palms, Rhaphis palms, Heliconia caribaea, Costus, Colocasia, Gardenia psidiodes, Opohiopogon japonicus, Plumeria obtuse, Heliconia lingulata, Ixora odorata

The orientation of the site influenced the landscape design. In strong winds the central courtyard becomes a sanctuary, with the residence acting as a buffer. Access to the property is via a small entry pavilion, which leads to a short garden path bordered with giant Lady Finger palms. The central axis of the garden path leads to a lawn featuring a giant lotus bowl. This is sheltered by a broad verandah and surrounded by the elegant 'Jade princess' palm, Medinilla speciosa and Peace lilies. Parallel to the entry path is the simple rectangular swimming pool. The innovative and striking planting design complements the existing coconut plantation sprawling below on the dunes.

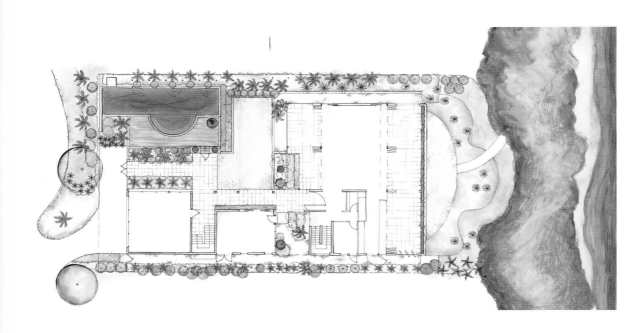

from left to right, above to below: sketch of house and garden, light floods into interior, path and lotus bowl, house protected by dense foliage

from above to below: architecture successfully blurs the boundary between inside and outside, coconut plantation sprawls along beachfront

from left to right: cool shaded seating area, tropical foliage disguises wall of the house

pool surrounded by lush green foliage

Sydney Garden

Sydney, Australia

Landscape architect: William Dangar + Associates
Architect: Thomas Rivard
Year of completion: 2009
Design elements used: pool, terraces
Plants: ivy, star jasmine, frangipani, russellia, orange trumpet vine

The site of this stunning garden is a steep slope with a series of terraces. Each terrace has its own landscape style, with a focus on tropical flowering plants, lush evergreen shrubs, and sculptural elements. The use of climbing plants as spillovers softens the architecture, and plants like ivy, star jasmine, and orange trumpet vine create green walls. Bamboo has been used on the boundary to create both privacy screening, and a green backdrop to the house. The secluded garden is a versatile and welcoming space providing a cool shady solace from the summer heat, and featuring a fire pit for cold winter nights.

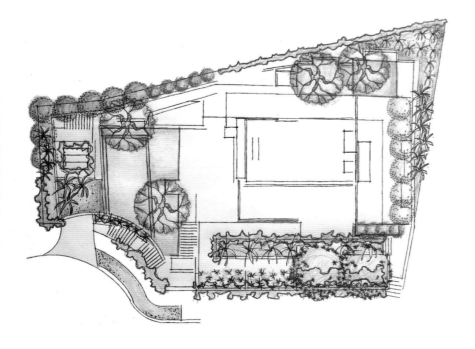

from left to right, above to below: garden and house plan, house with direct access to shady pool, seating area is an extension of interior living space

from above to below: potted plants and foliage embrace architecture,
house almost looks as if it is being reclaimed by nature

109

from left to right, above to below: native Canary Islands planting,
stepping stones, modernist planting urn

perspective view across the garden

Canary Islands Garden

London, United Kingdom

Landscape architect:
Amphibian Designs
Year of completion: 2009
Gross floor area: 150 m²
Design elements: Portland limestone, flamed black basalt, white lacquered timber
Plants: Aeonium arboreum, Dracaena draco, Echium pininana, Euphorbia mellifera, Senecio kleinia

Inspired by the rugged volcanic peaks and bizarre endangered flora of the Canary Island archipelago, this garden built at London's Chelsea Flower Show 2009 invited visitors to rediscover the forgotten face of this remote island chain. This thoroughly modern courtyard garden is designed to be set within the collapsed crater of an extinct island volcano. At its heart lies a moated pavilion, which

houses a thermal spa fed by naturally-heated spring water that rises up from deep within the crater. Here rough, black volcanic rock flanks sheets of thermal water, all surrounded by lush exotic planting. Cascades at the rear of the pavilion create an open-air spa shower, with a mineral Jacuzzi lying sunken within the moat.

111

from left to right, above to below: shade trellis, decking around stepping stone path, tranquil pond reflects plants and sky

from left to right, above to below: thermal bathing pools, planting, stepping stone path across thermal pools, house and garden plan

from above to below: rainforest planting, tree fern canopy

long perspective view across the garden

Tourism Malaysia Garden

London, United Kingdom

Landscape architect: Amphibian Designs
Year of completion: 2010
Gross floor area: 220 m²
Design elements: Portland limestone, western red cedar timber, living wall panels, black river pebbles
Plants: Asplenium nidus, Cyathea latebrosa, Ficus nitida, Pandanus amarilifolius, Raphis multifida

As the first-ever full-size tropical garden seen in the Chelsea Flower Show's 100 year history, this garden, designed for the villa of a holiday resort in Malaysia's Cameron Highlands, was commissioned by the Malaysian Tourism Board to promote the country as a key ecotourism destination. Inspired by lush rainforests and idyllic Kampung village gardens, this unashamedly modern design aimed to interpret Malaysia's diverse cultures and landscapes through a 21st century lens to create a garden as unusual, surprising and dynamic as the country itself.

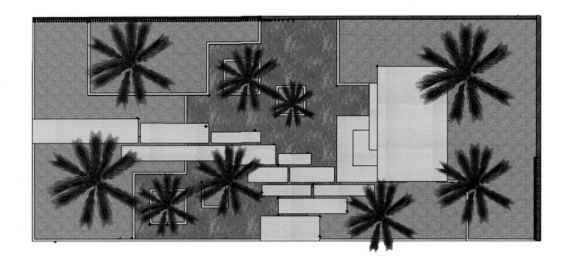

from left to right, above to below: house and garden plan, tree fern trunks contrast limestone path, back view of pavilion, close-up view of rainforest planting

from above to below: central pavilion, reflections of tree fern
canopies

from left to right, above to below: entrance to sunken pavilion, pavilion detail, stairs to sunken pavilion

pavilion surrounded by lilies

Tourism Malaysia Garden

London, United Kingdom

Landscape architect: Amphibian Designs
Year of completion: 2011
Gross floor area: 220 m²
Design elements: Portuguese brown limestone, walnut timber, tiger river pebbles
Plants: Alocasia cuprea, Livingstona rotundifolia, Nymphaea nouchali, Osmoxylon lineare, Schefflera puecklerii

This tropical garden designed for a modern residence in downtown Kuala Lumpur gained a coveted gold medal when built at London's Chelsea Flower Show in 2011. Inspired by the winding jungle streams and rich traditional architecture of the Malaysian archipelago, the scheme centered on a sunken seating pavilion surrounding by a snaking pool of fragrant tropical water lilies. Providing a modernist reworking of the 'flooded courtyard', a traditional Asian architectural design feature that uses sheets of water and lush planting to act as a natural air conditioning system, this highly functional scheme was designed not only to beautify but also to shade and cool the interior of a modern city residence in the tropics.

from left to right, above to below: pavilion nestles in plantings, roof detail, native plantings

from left to right, above to below: rare native Malaysian planting, ferns overhanging pool, tropical aquatic and riverine planting, house and garden plan

from left to right: welcoming entrance at dusk, palm trees create a more dramatic entrance

pergola, pool and landscape create a strong sense of presence

Coastal Modern Residence

Boca Grande, Florida, USA

Landscape architect:
DWY Landscape Architects
Architect: Thomas + Denzinger
Architects
Year of completion: 2011
Gross floor area: 1,500 m²
Design elements: Callida stone,
boardwalk,
lap pool, pergola
Plants: bamboo, travelers
palms, bromeliads, epiphytes,
zoysia grass, ferns

Located on a narrow strip of land between the Gulf of Mexico and an inter-coastal lagoon, this residence serves as a family gathering spot and seasonal escape for its owners. As such, the house was designed as two distinct pavilions separated by an elevated amenity level where the family could gather. The goal was not only to satisfy the program requirements with a landscape expression perceived as an extension of the architecture and site but, moreover, to do so in a dramatic and memorable way. The entrance connects the property across a private road while natural Callida stone articulates the open board fenestration of the home's exterior. Unique features of the landscape design include the use of epiphytes, a green wall, a boardwalk beneath the house with views through the pool, and an 30,000 liter cistern to collect rainwater for irrigation.

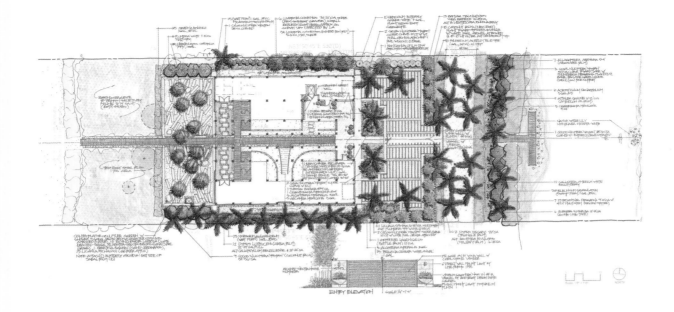

from left to right, above to below: site plan, pool with porch and spa, pool with fountain and terrace garden at sunset, tillandsia on a grid of stainless steel cable

above from left to right: striking entrance design, view from
terrace towards fresh water lagoon

from above to below: garden entrance, use of site-specific materials

house offers views over pool and garden

Coconut Grove

Coconut Grove, Florida, USA

Landscape architect: Raymond Jungles
Architect: Proun Space Studio
Year of completion: 2010
Design elements: oolite limestone, native plants
Plants: Sabal palms, bamboo, cycads, autograph tree, philodendron, Gumbo limbo, oil palm, Cuban petticoat palm, Lignum vitae, Zombie palm

The Coconut Grove garden is a family compound comprised of disparate styles and scales of architecture. Inspiration came from an existing eighty-year-old East Indian Banyan tree that crowned the ridge and straddled three different residential lots. The client's respect for the beauty of this tree made it a focal point of the property. The family compound has a continuous design language,

from the site-specific use of materials to the indigenous plantings and incorporation of water. Views through the Banyan tree's aerial prop roots reveal an elevated seating area that doubles as a stage for the client's fundraisers and private parties. The Fun Pool connects to the Fun House, which serves as a guest house and a gym.

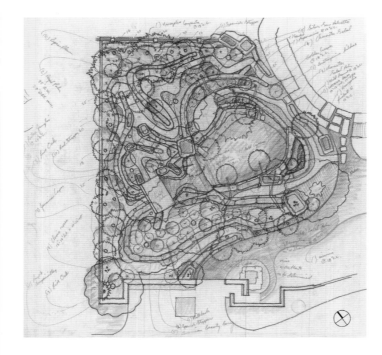

from left to right, above to below: elevated water feature plan, palm trees shading garden, water cascading into pool below, foliage lining winding walkway

from left to right, above to below: pool of water hidden gem in the dense foliage, garden has lots
of hidden landscape features, native plantings and trees offer privacy

from above to below: house surrounded by lush foliage, palm trees around house

white and blue of house contrast green foliage

Cornfeld Residence

Key West, Florida, USA

Landscape architect: Craig Reynolds Landscape Architecture
Architect: Bender and Associates
Year of completion: 2011
Gross floor area: 279 m²
Design elements: coral stone, green marble, fountains, Ipe wood decking
Plants: palms, pandanus specimen, Weeks hybrid philodendron, fern, blue flag iris

Homeowners from an ultra-contemporary home in Fort Lauderdale decided to try the other end of the spectrum in Key West. A classic grand dame of Key West architecture was purchased, with the intention of renovating it inside and out. A new pool with raised hot tub offers space to unwind. On one side is the raised Ipe hardwood deck and on the other side is a coral stone patio. A tropical oasis of new plantings surrounds the patio and backdrop of the pool. Three large Royal palms make a statement, forming a roof of sorts, while the focal point looking through the front door and out over the pool fountain is a collected pandanus specimen. Native and endangered Buccaneer palms and Coontie groundcover along with a single date palm and Aechmea Bromeliads round out the presentation.

from above to below: seating area hidden in foliage, private
pool with sundeck

from left to right, above to below: pool surrounded by paved path and plantings, white pool surround complements landscaping, detail of native plants, site plan

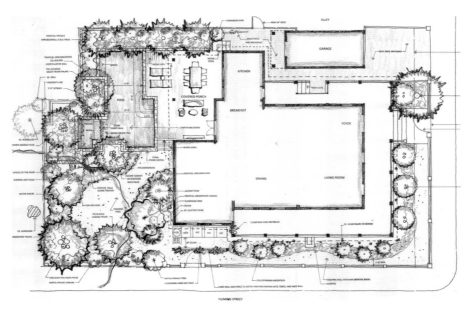

from left to right, above to below: home serves as outdoor living retreat, sunlit pool, seating

design inspired by idea of a pool in a clearing in the woods

Key West Retreat

Key West, Florida, USA

Landscape architect: Craig Reynolds Landscape Architecture
Architect: Thomas E. Pope
Year of completion: 2009
Gross floor area: 120 m²
Design elements: coral stone, Miami oolite stone, concrete, wood, local and carribean native plantings
Plants: palms, Coccothrinax alta, Zoysia grass, yellow lantana, Latania palm

This project began as an empty lot, purchased by the client who then intended to turn it into a vacation home that would serve as a winter getaway. The owner requested a garden-centered home with a pool, deep porches and plenty of sunshine. With that idea in mind, the home was placed in the front left corner of the property, leaving as much space as possible for a pool and garden. The inspiration for the garden came from the notion of a clearing in the woods with a pond. A place where you could enter and feel the sky all the way down to the water while being surrounded by plants. This Key West garden is a retreat for outdoor living that is both beautiful and functional.

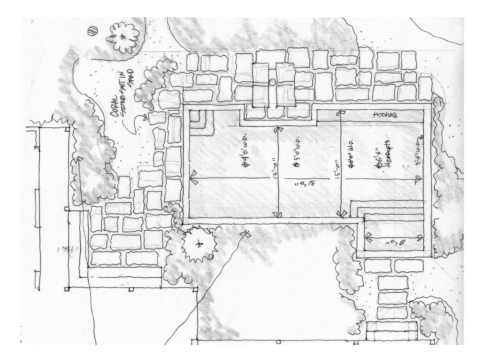

from above to below: pool site plan, hammock surrounded by foliage

from left to right, above to below: paved walkway winds
through foliage, pool detail, sun loungers by pool

137

from left to right: water garden hidden by dense foliage, planting
detail

water garden

El Palmar

Coral Gables, Florida, USA

Landscape architect: Raymond Jungles
Architect: Cesar Molina
Year of completion: 2006
Design elements: oolite limestone, native plant material, concrete, water features
Plants: orchids, baobob tree, golden creeper, philodendron, papyrus, bougainvillea, bailey palms, oil palms, rainbow eucalyptus tree

The clients wanted their house to reflect the haciendas of their Cuban homeland, complete with royal palms, a generous lawn, and tropical nuances. Cesar Molina's tropical colonial-style architecture is well suited to the subtropical climate. A sizeable trellis runs perpendicular to the street and is covered with flowering vines that veil views of the house. In the center of the generous courtyard, a large rectangular oolite monolith carved to function as a bubbling water basin is flanked by Chambeyronia palms with Vanda orchids attached to their trunks. The pool and garden patio are at the level of the house. Palms shade the pool and patios, minimizing paving. Views across the pool area and down the long wide waterway influenced the placement of the widest portions of the pool deck.

from left to right, above to below: landscaping combines clearings
and foliage, house surrounded by plants, water garden

from above to below: palm trees, harmony between dense foliage
and taller trees, site plan

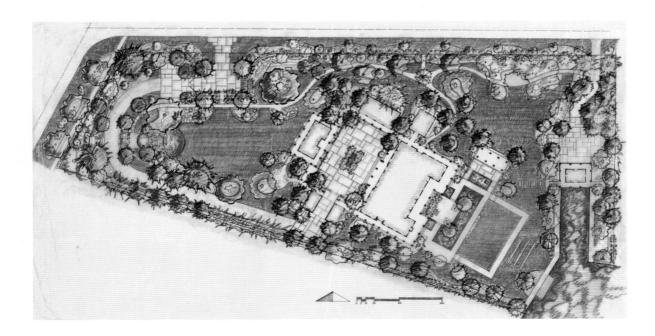

from above to below: foliage offers privacy, dense greenery open out above winding pathways

design fuses interior and exterior spaces

Lazenby Garden

Miami, Florida, USA

Landscape architect: Raymond Jungles
Architect: Mark Hampton
Year of completion: 2009
Design elements: native plants, stacked slate, river rock, concrete
Plants: bromeliads, live oak trees, orchids, staghorn ferns, licuala palms, golden creeper, philodendron, ferns

The design of the Lazenby Garden creates a seamless living environment by fusing interior and exterior spaces. Upon entering, shadows take form and fall gracefully upon the garden spaces, pool and water element. The clients wanted to create a new entrance sequence. To achieve this, the driveway was pushed further away from the front door in order to make space for a ceremonial garden entry to the home. This was achieved through a wooden deck around an existing mahogany tree and elevated asymmetric concrete platforms pressed with rock salt, giving depth and texture. The outdoor areas present many different views into the garden, where a meditative aura reigns. Much thought was given as to what forms the pool's surface would reflect in the daytime, what natural and artificial light would reflect at night, and how the reflections would fall.

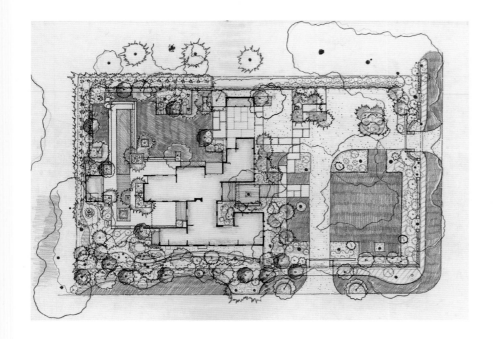

from left to right, above to below: site plan, shady path winds through garden, pool, water cascades down water feature

from above to below: private pool, pool shaded by dense foliage

from left to right, above to below: sunlit terrace, upper deck offers
a relaxing place to enjoy the views, modern living space

terrace offers a stunning area for dining and relaxing

Rock House

Miami, Florida, USA

Landscape architect: Max Strang Architecture
Architect: Max Strang Architecture
Year of completion: 2004
Gross floor area: 511 m²
Design elements: oolitic limestone, steel, ipe wood, Florida keystone
Plants: Florida strangler fig, live oak, Royal poinciana, Royal palm, bamboo, coconut palm

Architect Max Strang designed Rock House as a family retreat within the dense landscape of Coconut Grove, Miami's oldest neighborhood. The result was a seamless merging of architecture and landscape. The entire upper floor is inspired by the tropical designs of the late Sri Lankan architect Geoffrey Bawa. The exposed rusted steel roof provides a modernist edge to the overall aesthetic. The lower floor of the home is clad entirely with local oolitic limestone, the local bedrock of South Florida. The pool was excavated amidst the ruins of a small cottage that was formerly on the property. Orchids grow from the low stone foundation walls and occasionally drop flowers into the black bottomed pool. Although technically located in a subtropical climate, Rock House proves that the 'tropics' are alive and well in Miami.

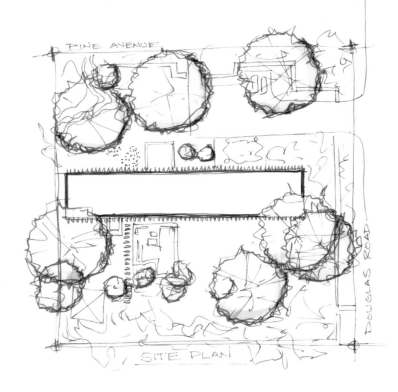

from left to right, above to below: sketch of garden and house, beautiful pool surrounded by lush foliage, oolite detail, papyrus

from left to right, above to below: rear of Rock House, statue,
breathtaking garden view

from above to below: stream winds its way through foliage,
stream hidden by native plantings

water feature surrounded by lush green plantings

Gile Residence

Sugarloaf Key, Florida, USA

Landscape architect:
Craig Reynolds Landscape
Architecture
Architect: Michael Ingram
Year of completion: 2008
Gross floor area: 21,780 m²
Design elements: North Caro-
lina river rock and brick
Plants: Coccothrinax alta, Royal
palms, Philodron magnifica,
papyrus, Canna lily, Textilis
bamboo, kentia and Fiji island
fan palms

The owner of this property wanted to transform an empty front yard, open to the street, into his own private tropical oasis. The design was inspired by a garden with a stream, pond and meandering paths – reminiscent of a great tropical hotel garden he once visited. The idea was to get lost in a shaded tropical palm forest with the ever-present sound of a stream. The design culminated in a winding network of pathways with large fronds purposely set close to the walkways, hiding what was around the next bend. Palms such as kentia, silver thatch, white elephant palm, and Coccothrinax alta were artfully set around the centerpiece – a large pond and cascading stream full of iris, papyrus, and water lilies.

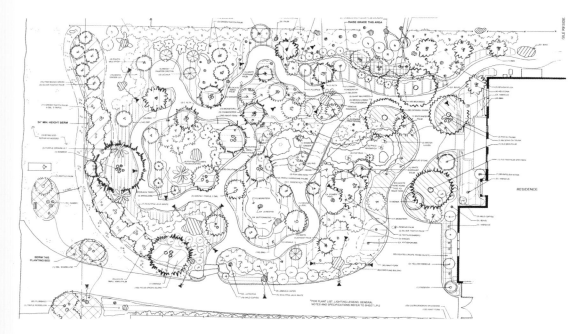

from left to right, above to below: site plan, trees shade path, trees offer shade from the sun, bright flowers complement green foliage

from left to right, above to below: stone surround gives pool its natural appearance,
stream creates a clearing in the dense foliage, lilies and native plants in stream

from left to right: an abstraction of a Hawaiian 'piko' adorns the entry gates, the master bedroom appears to float in the pool

an ocean of lawn welcomes the cooling trade winds and is an elegant setting for entertaining

Tropical Craftman's Home

Kona, Hawaii, USA

Landscape architect: Vita Planning & Landscape Architecture
Architect: de Reus Architects
Year of completion: 2004
Gross floor area: 6,070 m²
Design elements: circular motor court, entry fountain, private bath gardens, great lawn, multi-level pools
Plants: palms, trees, shrubs, groundcovers, vines, perennials, herbs

This private residence on the Big Island of Hawaii is surrounded by pools with thin stone coping that visually disappears to form an interpretation of the natural edge between the land and water. In the traditional style of Hawaiian outdoor living, this house is composed of multiple buildings arranged by function and connected by paths through tropical gardens. A striking water feature and a tunnel of areca palms direct visitors towards the main house past narrow hidden paths to guest cottages and a home office. Along with the social spaces of the main house, there are many intimate, private spaces around the pool and in the gardens outside the guest cottages.

from left to right, above to below: Asian sculpture in private
bath garden, multi-level pool, garden and pool appear as an
extension of the house

from left to right, above to below: partially submerged pool chairs provide respite from the tropical heat, a stone tiger guards the entrance, a 'cathedral' of palms arching over the entry walk, site plan

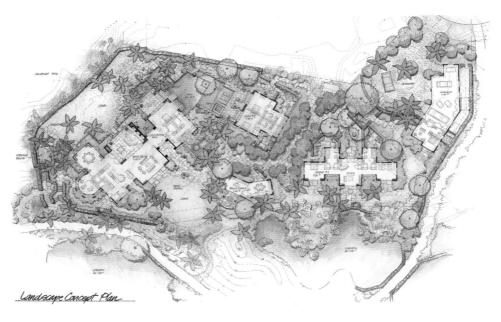

Landscape Concept Plan

from above to below: foliage continues right to boundary of property, pool with waterfall

pool inspired by idea of a forest clearing

Sisson Residence

Miami, Florida, USA

Landscape architect: Craig Reynolds Landscape Architecture
Architect: Matthew Stratton
Year of completion: 2004
Gross floor area: 511 m²
Design elements: oolitic limestone, steel, ipe wood, Florida keystone
Plants: Florida strangler fig, live oak, Royal poinciana, Royal palm, bamboo, coconut palm

A relatively unused side yard was transformed into a shaded, tropical oasis. A lagoon-style pool with deep green pebble-stone finish and Tennessee ledge rocks have been combined with old Chicago brick to create a centerpiece. The canopy surrounds are anchored by three large Royal palms. Ledge rocks that double up as benches create a dynamic elevation change on this relatively flat site. A backdrop of native saw palmetto and the fragrant cinnamon bark tree create privacy for a hidden outdoor shower. A back walkway near the owners second master suite outdoor shower has been kept deliberately separate. It meanders in the shade of the black calabash and tall palms.

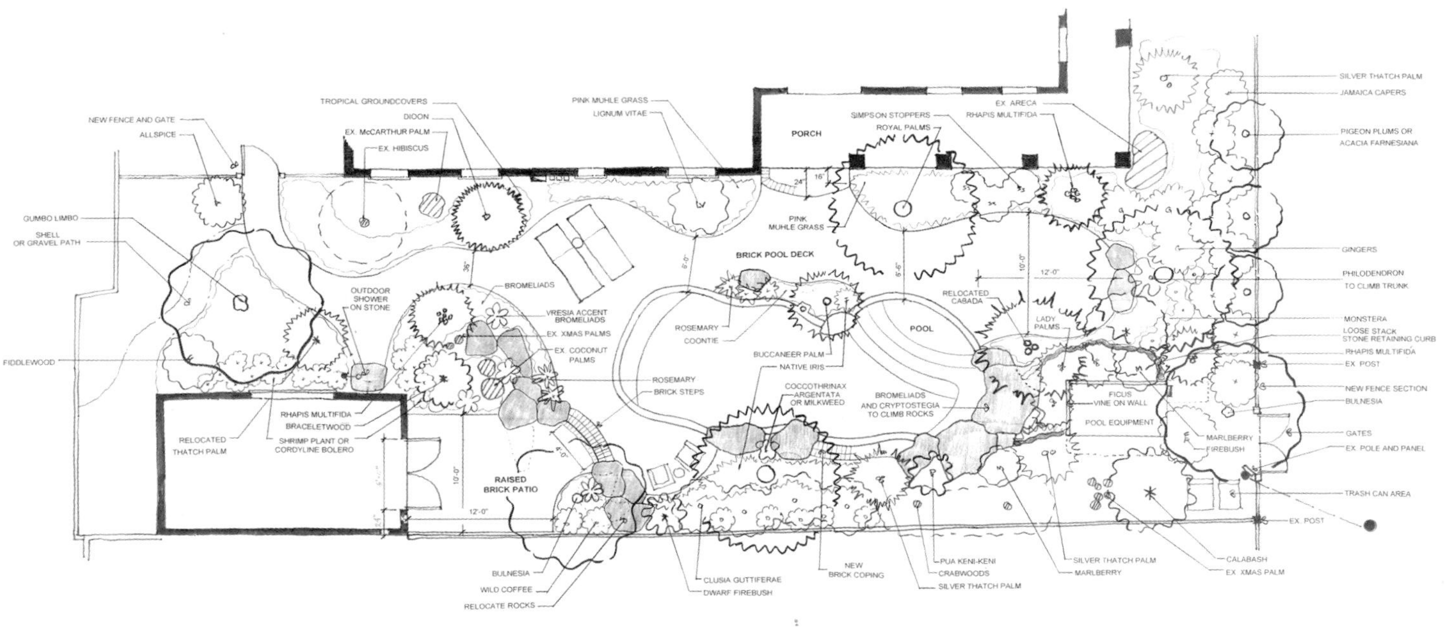

TROPICAL GROUNDCOVERS
DIOON
EX. McCARTHUR PALM
EX. HIBISCUS
NEW FENCE AND GATE
ALLSPICE
PINK MUHLE GRASS
LIGNUM VITAE
PORCH
SIMPSON STOPPERS
ROYAL PALMS
EX. ARECA
RHAPIS MULTIFIDA
SILVER THATCH PALM
JAMAICA CAPERS
PIGEON PLUMS OR ACACIA FARNESIANA
GUMBO LIMBO
SHELL OR GRAVEL PATH
PINK MUHLE GRASS
BRICK POOL DECK
GINGERS
PHILODENDRON TO CLIMB TRUNK
OUTDOOR SHOWER ON STONE
BROMELIADS
VRESIA ACCENT BROMELIADS
EX. XMAS PALMS
EX. COCONUT PALMS
ROSEMARY
COONTIE
RELOCATED CABADA
LADY PALMS
POOL
MONSTERA
LOOSE STACK STONE RETAINING CURB
RHAPIS MULTIFIDA
EX. POST
FIDDLEWOOD
BUCCANEER PALM
NATIVE IRIS
ROSEMARY
BRICK STEPS
COCCOTHRINAX ARGENTATA OR MILKWEED
BROMELIADS AND CRYPTOSTEGIA TO CLIMB ROCKS
FICUS VINE ON WALL
POOL EQUIPMENT
NEW FENCE SECTION
BULNESIA
RHAPIS MULTIFIDA
BRACELETWOOD
SHRIMP PLANT OR CORDYLINE BOLERO
RELOCATED THATCH PALM
MARLBERRY
FIREBUSH
GATES
EX. POLE AND PANEL
RAISED BRICK PATIO
12'-0"
10'-0"
TRASH CAN AREA
EX. POST
BULNESIA
WILD COFFEE
RELOCATE ROCKS
CLUSIA GUTTIFERAE
DWARF FIREBUSH
NEW BRICK COPING
PUA KENI-KENI
CRABWOODS
SILVER THATCH PALM
SILVER THATCH PALM
MARLBERRY
CALABASH
EX. XMAS PALM

from left to right, above to below: pool area plan, walkway winds through foliage, landscaping meets house, planting detail

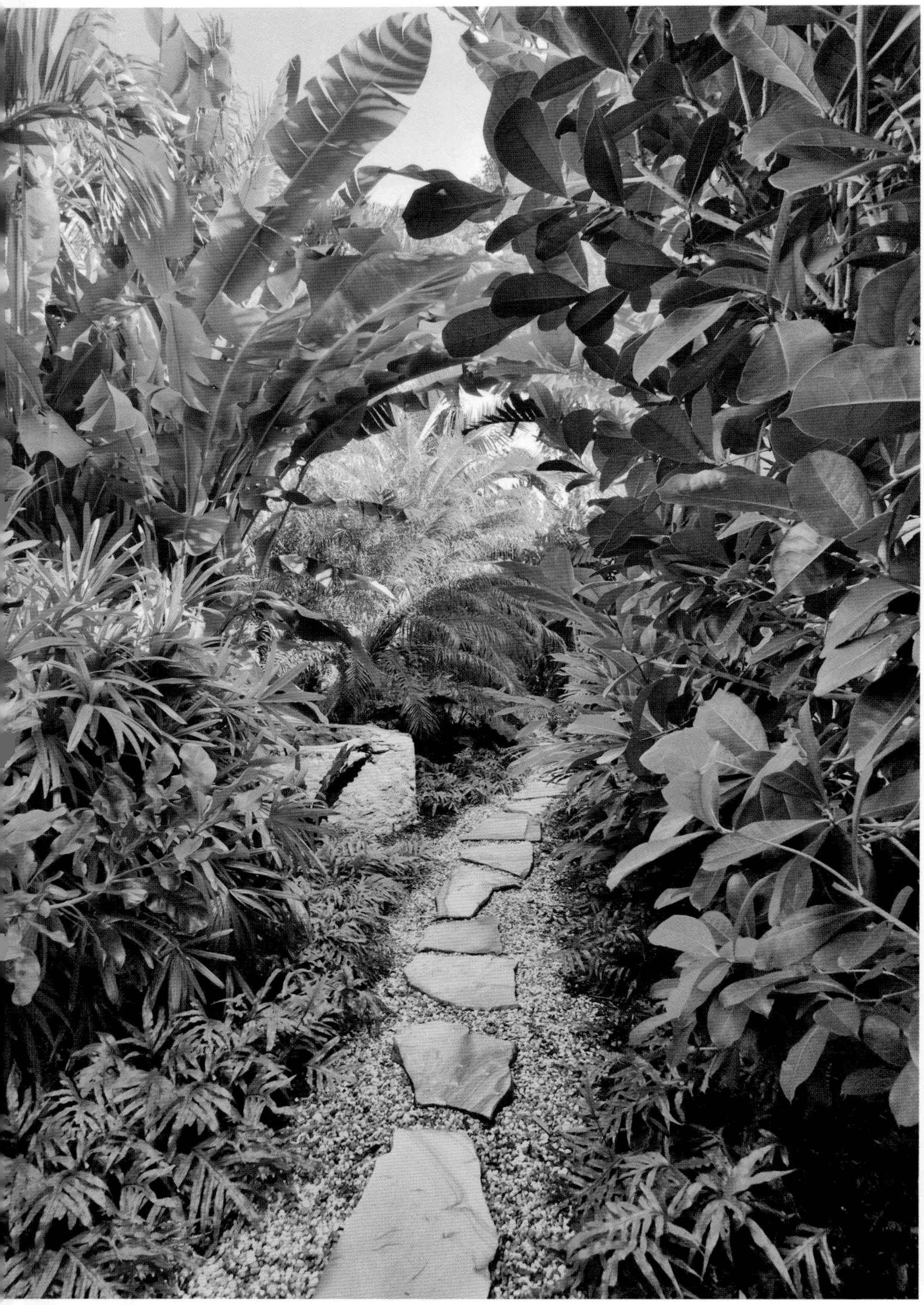

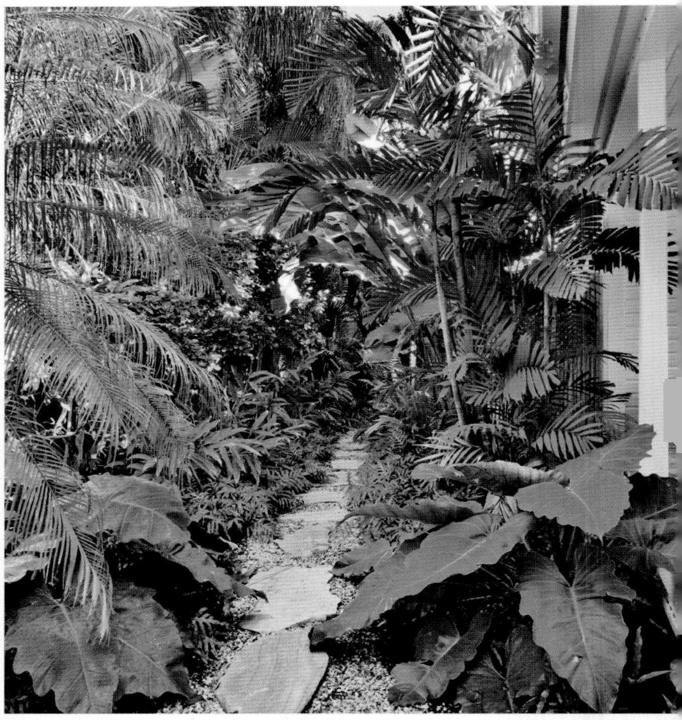

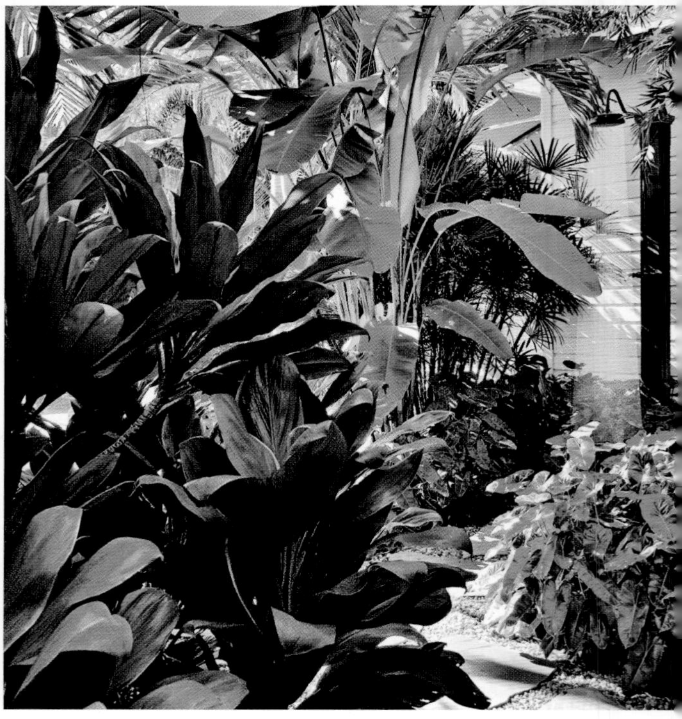

from left to right, above to below: pool offers shady place to relax,
foliage offers privacy, surroundings reflected in pool surface

from above to below: beautiful pool area with boulders, pool with mountain views and surrounding palm trees

water feature in tranquil setting

Albi Estate

Paradise Valley, California, USA

Landscape architect: Exteriors by Chad Robert
Year of completion: 2006
Gross floor area: 6,880 m²
Design elements: hand-carved cantera stone pots, fountains, antique floor tiles, tropical plants
Plants: Phoenix dactylifera 'Medjool', Phoenix canariensis, Chamaerops humilis, citrus, agaves species

This garden was designed to become a series of collections, inspired by the homeowner's favorite travel destinations and pastimes. Maximizing the excellent views of the mountains and Arizona sunsets, the designs of the individual gardens include references to an Andalusian courtyard, an Italian villa, a moonlight garden, and a butterfly and hummingbird garden, creating a strikingly diverse collection of gardens for the owner. The spaces are each unique in feeling and style yet they seem to flow effortlessly into each other and create a cohesive composition. The selection of the boulders used on the project was somewhat challenging as the color needed to be a near perfect match to the distant mountains, in order to 'connect' the mountain to the garden. The swimming pool was designed to create a tranquil space, which would reflect views of the mountains.

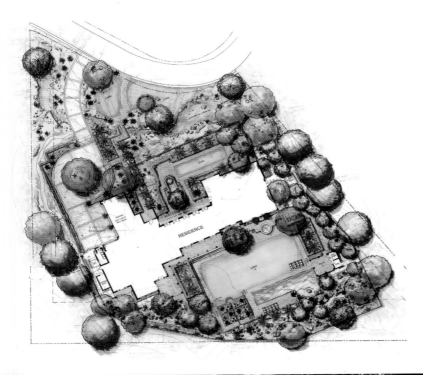

from left to right, above to below: concept plan, glass water feature, front garden with stunning mountain backdrop, tropical planting

from above to below: water feature in front of planted
terraces, elegant Mediterranean courtyard

from above to below: sun-drenched pool, sunny lounge area next to pool

front entrance flanked by palm trees

Valley Vista Estate

Paradise Valley, California, USA

Landscape architect: Exteriors by Chad Robert
Architect: Carson Poetzl Architects
Year of completion: 2009
Gross floor area: 9,712 m²
Design elements: Italian travertine, brick, Cantera stone, pebbles, mosaic tiles
Plants: citrus, date palms, Mediterranean fan palms, native plants from the Sonoran desert

This tropical oasis is reminiscent of the architecture of southern Spain. The white stucco walls, red-tiled roofs, hand carved stone detailing, and the use of Moorish tile, are typical of this architectural style. The rear garden was remodeled to include a new swimming pool and spa with Moroccan tile accents. The streets and courtyards of Cordoba, Spain inspired the detailed tiles and mosaic pebble work on the entry walk and steps. The primary entry to the residence is flanked by two private courtyards; one with a strong Moorish theme, Moorish style fireplace, fountain and covered dining terrace. The master bathroom courtyard has its own private fireplace and the outdoor rug was created with thousands of tiny white and black pebbles individually hand set.

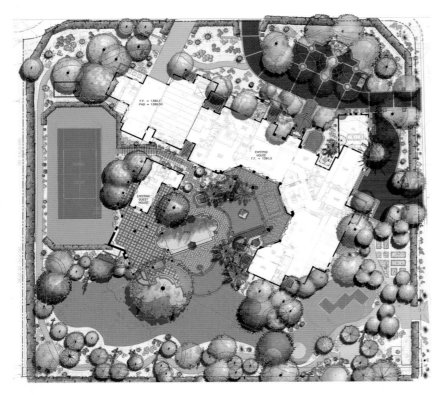

from left to right, above to below: concept plan, water feature and fireplace, fire pit

from left to right, above to below: pool shaded by palm trees,
palm trees shade front entrance

from left to right, above to below: sheltered terrace with views of pool and garden, pool surrounded by dense foliage, coconut palm detail

garden incorporated into architecture

Latterner Residence

Miami, Florida, USA

Landscape architect: Max Strang
Architecture
Architect: Max Strang
Architecture
Year of completion: 2008
Gross floor area: 3,500 m²
Design elements: pool,
open terraces
Plants: ginger, heliconias, oyster
plants, philodendron, oak trees,
frangipani, coconut palm

Ensconced in the subtropical wildness of Miami's Coconut Grove, the Latterner Residence conjures up images of a modernist spa carved out of the jungle. The surrounding garden is dominated by an "anything grows" design strategy. Amidst the green chaos, a fragrant frangipani tree searches for sunlight and occasionally drops its flowers into the water below. From the pool deck, a natural path descends into a cool grotto. The permanence of the home's architecture offers a stark contrast to the ever-changing foliage that surrounds it.

from left to right, above to below: site plan, covered terrace gives respite from the sun, pool shaded by trees

garden is a tropical paradise

from above to below: beautiful contrast of orange and greens, boulders used to define different garden areas

from left to right, above to below: water courses add to the sensual experience, entrance, design incorporates many indigenous species

Golden Rock Inn

Nevis, West Indies

Landscape architect: Raymond Jungles, Inc.
Architect: Ed Tuttle
Year of completion: 2011
Design elements: boulders, native plants, water features, water gardens
Plants: bromeliads, philodendron, cabada palm, bougainvillea, kalanchoe, walking iris

The site of the Golden Rock Inn is perched over 300 meters above sea level on the lower side of Mount Nevis, an inactive volcano. The stewards of this intimate hotel, both artists, were attracted to the historic site by the abundance of living things sharing the grounds. Creating the necessary terraces and roads for the new restaurant approach unearthed boulders, stones, and pebbles; these were set aside and later arranged to retain steep slopes, build steps, and create water retention. The artists' love of lush, wild vegetation directed the usage of many indigenous species, as well as colorful subtropical species from around the world. All of the elements that define the art of garden creation are in harmony; light, stone, water, plants, structure, landform, and sky. Stunning views towards Montserrat and Antigua complete the sensual experience of this wind-blown mountainside retreat.

from left to right, above to below: pathway meandering through lush foliage, lawn is like a clearing in the forest, sunlight filtering through dense wild foliage

from left to right, above to below: stunning mountain scenery creates the perfect backdrop, steps leading to vantage point, lush wild vegetation, section drawn by Raymond Jungles

from left to right: palms separate property from beach, seating
area

shaded pool with views of beach

Davids Garden

Treasure Cay, Bahamas

Landscape architect: Raymond Jungles
Year of completion: 2009
Design elements: native plant material, water features, walkways, pool
Plants: sabal palm, philodendron, bromeliads, bay cedar, beach dune sunflower, golden creeper, Dominican sabal palm, native grasses

Davids Garden is an imaginative study on what can be planted in the toughest of Bahamian beachfront elements. Water creates a link between the different landscaped areas by lapping the sea lavender-draped shoreline; spilling from the infinity edge pool and reflecting the sculpted overhanging rock formations of the entry garden streams. The landscape architects utilized the entire site as well as the borrowed beachfront landscape to create a visual and an auditory garden dialogue. The garden was designed to require minimal maintenance and withstand the elements; harsh sun, salt spray, and sea breeze. As visitors enter the garden from the heavily planted roadway, they walk on a boardwalk through and over four water features, with a series of waterfalls, streams and bridges connected by an old nautical rope discovered during one of the client's fishing excursions.

from left to right, above to below: pool almost appears to join the sea, privat
pool surrounded by dense foliage, pool at night

from left to right, above to below: design blurs boundary between natural and manmade, cascading water, foliage borders beach, site plan

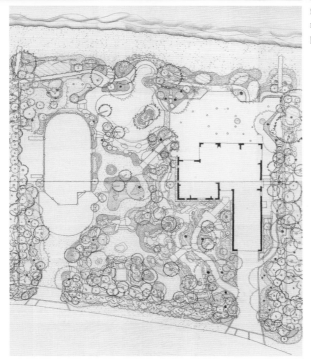

from left to right, above to below: shaded terrace with breathtaking views of beach, roofed terrace with views of pool and garden, foliage surrounds house

shaded seating areas and dense foliage open out to the beach

Iporanga House

Guarujá, Brazil

Landscape architect: Leo Laniado
Architect: Isay Weinfeld
Year of completion: 2006
Gross floor area: 875 m²
Design elements: pool, sheltered seating areas, terrace
Plants: Etlingera elatior, Gardenia jasminoides, Myrtus communis, Vriesea imperialis, Heliconia rostrata, Calliandra harrisi, Dietes bicolor, Alpinia zerumbet

Built on the seashore of Iporanga beach, on the north coast of São Paulo and amidst the Atlantic Forest, Iporanga House is surrounded by vegetation – coconut trees, bromeliads and other indigenous plants from the region. No walls surround the house, and the only protection comes from green fences separating it from the neighboring lots or the beach. The program is distributed in two white box-like volumes, one placed over the other;

the lower one houses living and dining rooms, which open out towards the veranda, the swimming pool and the sea. In the upper volume, a large 'musharabiya' made of aluminum and painted in white encloses all five bedrooms – the master bedroom has stunning views of the sea. Outside by the swimming pool is a lowered sitting room that can be covered with a canvas, a place where one can have lunch or just relax.

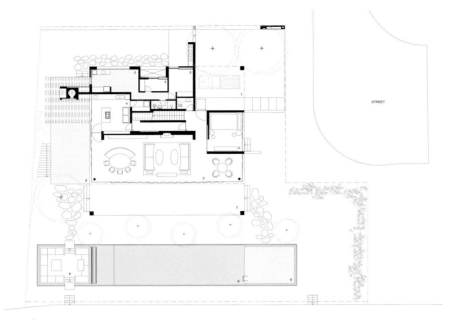

from left to right, above to below: house and garden plan, private seating area, pool hidden from beach by greenery, terrace opens to garden and blurs the boundaries between inside and outside

from above to below: covered area with sandy floor, architecture seeks to incorporate
nature into the design and is open towards the garden and beach

from left to right: pathway winds through the dense foliage, foliage embraces the pool area giving it a natural look

large glass doors and windows offer superb views of pool and garden from both sides

Casa Gêneses

São Paulo, Brazil

Landscape architect:
Isabel Duprat
Architect: Isay Weinfeld
Year of completion: 2011
Gross floor area: 2,700 m²
Design elements: pool
Plants: Raphidophora decursiva, Arachis repers, Zoysia japonica, Brunfeisia uniflora, Ficus pumila, and others

This project has been organized on three levels; concentrating the flat landscaped areas, swimming pool and social rooms at the highest level. The wide main room that takes up the full extension of the level is marked by three strong vertical references: a fireplace and two round pillars clad in stainless steel. The glass doors on either side of the room open completely onto two verandas. A red cube contains a Japanese-style dining room, which projects outwards onto one of the verandas. The circulation follows a long internal hallway, or a terraced balcony cantilevered over the garden, onto which all bedrooms open. On its main façade, the house reveals a balanced composition between the closed surface of the outer wall, the lines of the concrete structure, and the strips of glass of the window frames, in contrast to the red block of the small Japanese-style dining room.

from left to right, above to below: overhanging upper story reduces house foot
print, foliage cleared around house to create an open garden, red extension b
fully contrasts greenery

from above to below: architectural design seeks to incorporate nature, open-plan design and large windows maximize views, ground floor plan

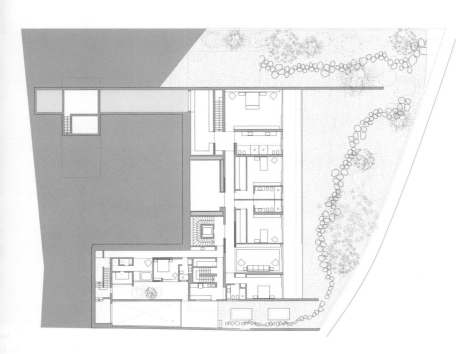

from above to below: a place to explore and make discoveries, pool surrounded by dense foliage

design blends nature with manmade

DS Residence

São Paulo, Brazil

Landscape architect: Gil Fialho
Architect: Arthur Casas
Year of completion: 2008
Gross floor area: 450 m²
Design elements: pool, designer benches
Plants: Calathea lutea, Pandanus utilis, Monstera deliciosa, Costus spicatus, Alpinia purpurata, Etlingera hemisphaerica, Heliconia collinsiana, Arundina bambusifolia, Alcantarea imperialis

Idealized by the owner's dream, this landscape project invites the visitor to reflect and contemplate their surroundings. The entrance has a mysterious feel, surrounded by a giant Calathea lutea and Pandanus utilis path, the garden is something to be explored along the way. Groups of heliconias and alpinias cover the walls along the trajectory; framing the glass wall of the living room. By the pool, monsteras and costus protect the rocky wall. Finally, benches from designer Hugo França invite the users to take a break and appreciate the tropical beauty of this stunning garden paradise.

from above to below: house and garden plan, foliage planted right
up to the house

from left to right, above to below: pool seating area, trees and plants shade paved path, hidden path winds around house, garden offers secret places to sit and relax

from left to right: house with views of pool and garden, vines taper up
house walls blurring the boundary between architecture and nature

garden embraces house walls

Pedro Useche House

São Paulo, Brazil

Landscape architect: Gil Fialho
Architect: Pedro Useche
Year of completion: 2005
Gross floor area: 2,095 m²
Design elements: pool, decking, Portuguese mosaic
Plants: alpinias, zingibers, Hysophorbe lagenicaulis, Pandanus utilis, Phyllostachys edulis, Arachis repens, Archontophoenix cunninghamii, Bauhinias falcata, Crinum asiaticum

This project began with an analysis of the terrain and architectural character of the house. The landscape designers then devised a model of the principles and volumetric areas of the proposed landscaped area. The idea was that the garden would involve the frontal part of the residence, transforming the entrance into a green curtain that embraces the entire façade, protecting the house from the sun. The entrance of the garden is a combination of Hysophorbe lagenicaulis and Pandanus utilis, together with filondendros and banana trees. The stairs that access the social entrance are covered by Arachis repens between the steps. By the pool, the landscape combines Archontophoenix cunninghamii, which is beautifully reflected on the surface of the pool. On the right side there is a small orchard that feeds the birds and supplies fruits for occasional Caipirinha cocktails.

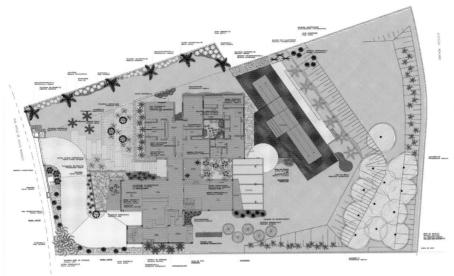

from left to right, above to below: site and house plan, dense foliage, architecture blurs the boundary between inside and outside

from above to below: protective porch in front of house, patio
offers a shady place to relax and enjoy the view

from left to right, above to below: house surrounded by lush
foliage, sandy garden has a real tropical feel, open-plan interior

gallery surrounds all three floors of the house

Casa Tropical

Mundaú, Brazil

Landscape architect:
Camarim Arquitectos
Architect:
Camarim Arquitectos
Year of completion: 2008
Gross floor area: 2,400 m²
Design elements: open gallery
Plants: coconut trees, mango trees, papaya trees, guava trees

Mundaú is a fishing village located on the coast in the state of Ceará, in north-east Brazil. The clients wanted a holiday house with three bedrooms that offered lots of possibilities for close contact with nature. A gallery surrounds the three floors of the house. Both the wooden skin that envelops the gallery and the suspended roof, shelter the house from the sun while keeping it permeable to the cool south wind. The open roof leaves space for high glass panels, merging coconut trees, dunes and sea with the open-plan interior. The landscape design comprises a series of interventions that transformed the agricultural land into a tropical garden. Parallel irrigation channels, were redesigned as long diagonals across the garden. Granite stones demarcate special areas: a table under a passion fruit pergola, a street access under the shadow of an old cashew tree, and a lush green hideaway.

199

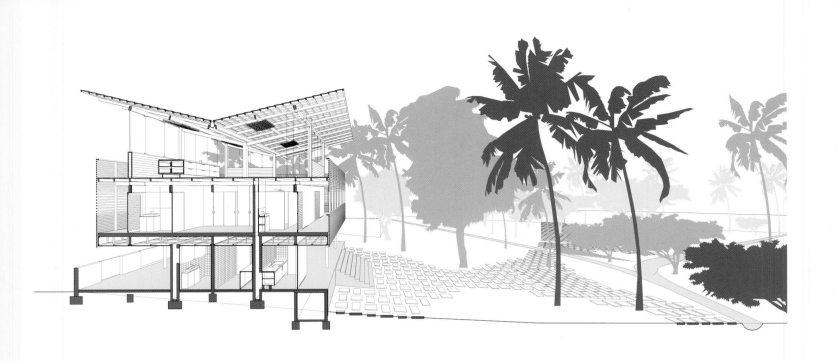

from above to below: section, stairs linking galleries

from left to right, above to below: wooden lattices give house a very open appearance,
kitchen with views over garden, gallery breaches the gap between interior and exterior

from left to right, above to below: space designed to invite and
intrigue visitors, sun-drenched terrace, pavilion provides a shady
spot to relax

from left to right, above to below: design uses many different textures, garden full of surprises, wooden terraces act like clearings in a forest

Casa Cor

São Paulo, Brazil

Landscape architect: Alex Hanazaki Landscaping
Architect: Sajous
Year of completion: 2006
Gross floor area: 900 m²
Design elements: terraces, pavilions
Plants: Myrciaria cauliflora, Prunus serrulata, Dracaena sanderiana, Cycas revoluta, Phoenix roebelenii, Philodendron speciosum, Philodendron bipinnatifidium

This is a garden capable of surprising and stimulating all the senses: smell, touch, hearing, taste and sight. The space is deliberately inviting and designed to intrigue the visitor. The design concept awakens the sense of sight through the architectural layout, which creates a counter point between orthogonal volume and organic forms. Touch is stimulated by the various textures present in materials and in the vegetation used. A cacophony of different smells are exuded by the huge variety of plants and flowers. Hearing is awakened by the sound of water coming from the water mirror and the fountain. Taste is stimulated by existing edible fruit trees. The lighting concept creates gives the environment a scenic character, with some help from discreet appliances and fixtures, which are almost invisible to the eye.

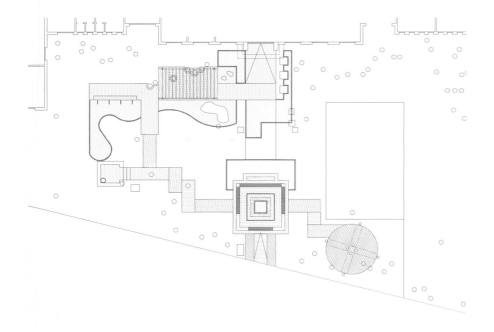

from left to right, above to below: site and house plan, walls and paving break up the dense foliage, garden stimulates all the senses

from left to right, above to below: path winds from house through garden, palm trees shade and protect the garden
from the tropical sun, range of high trees and low shrubs gives garden an exciting and varied appearance

from left to right, above to below: architecture blurs the boundary between i
and outside, pool hidden amongst palm trees, garden with ocean views

huge variety of plant species included in garden design

Ilhabela

São Paulo, Brazil

Landscape architect: Alex Hanazaki Landscaping
Architect: Suzana Scherman
Year of completion: 2012
Gross floor area: 2,000 m²
Design elements: pool, projecting roof, terraces, wooden decking
Plants: Agapanthus africanus, Costus stenophyllus, Gunnera manicata, Xanthosoma robustum, Hoya carnosa, Aquaticas, Ninfea

Spread across approximately 2,000 square meters of land, the huge variety of tropical plants used to create this garden paradise guarantees the exuberant character of this site, facing the sea. The path is made of recycled brick and indicates way to the large wooden deck of Itaúba wood, where loungers and tables offer a space for family and friends to relax and interact surrounded by beautiful views of the sea. A large reflecting pool lined with stones runs along the sloping terrain bringing the soft sound of trickling water to the space.

from left to right, above to below: pool loungers with views of the sea, a spa for soaking up the sun and enjoying the views, house incorporates tradition architectural features

from left to right, above to below: romantic setting, pool surrounded by dense foliage, architcture uses traditional techniques, site and garden plan

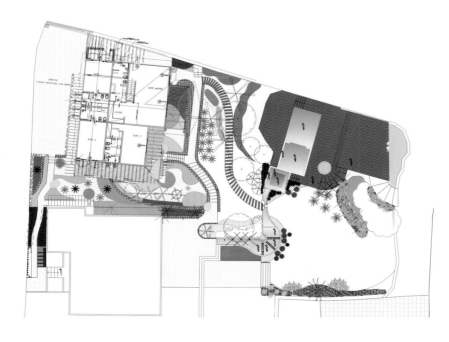

from left to right, above to below: breathtaking views from main villa, main entrance uses traditional architectural elements, house appears to glow in the evening light

perfectly positioned sun deck

Villa Mayana

Playa Dominical, Costa Rica

Landscape architect:
Rick Olswanger
Architect: Joaristi & Barascout
Year of completion: 2007
Gross floor area: 1,500 m²
Design elements: palm leaves,
wood, unpolished marble
Plants: palm trees, Bismarckia
nobilis, Phenakospermum
guyannense, ginger, Codiaeum
variegatum, bromelias,
Monstera deliciosa

Located in Playa Dominical on the south coast of Costa Rica, this project results from formal research about contemporary architecture developed along tropical borders from America to Australia, through Africa and Asia. Such learning has resulted in the development of a truly memorable design perfectly suited to a tropical climate.

The project details majestic heights in ceilings with outlet openings to ensure warm air outflows. Pronounced eaves give shelter from sun and rain, and the use of piles in the structure separate it from the soil, allowing air to flow beneath. The sloping terrain is used to form terraces that make the most of the mountain panorama.

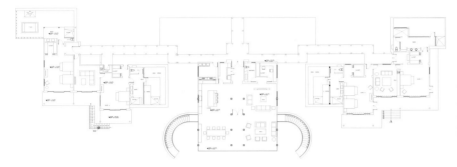

from left to right, above to below: ground floor plan, terraces and pavilion overlooking large pool, water gardens and pools act almost as an extension of the house, foliage is cleared around the pool permitting views of the mountain terrain

from left to right, above to below: bright dining area, decorative
plant pots bring nature inside, stunning views over pool

from left to right, above to below: Washingtonia palms and pathway bordered by lime trees, cascading waterfall, straight lines create a light and shadow effect in the design of the garden

from left to right, above to below: water feature in front of house, plants alongside water feature, pool surrounded by olive trees and native palms alongside a rill reminiscent of the Arabian gardens in Andalusia

Anda Dar

Marrakesh, Morocco

Landscape architect: Philippe Dubreuil Jardiniste
Architect: Hakim BenJelloun
Year of completion: 2004
Gross floor area: 10,000 m²
Design elements: pool, cascading water features
Plants: olive trees, Washington palm, lime trees, atriplex, Pennisetum alopecuroides, agave, bougainvillea, mioporum, fig trees

Like an oasis rising out of the desert, this garden was planted from scratch, on a site previously occupied by just a few palm trees. An old ruined building was used as a base for the pool. The client, together with the landscape designer and architect, determined the site for the house. The landscaping design involves paths and straight lines, which have the effect of making the garden look larger.

Raised walls and a cascading waterfall help to hide the house from view. The garden is designed to optimize the stunning views of the surrounding landscape and also uses water features, sculptures and varying scents to stimulate the senses and create a vivid, intriguing space in which to relax.

from left to right, above to below: pool surrounded by high walls offers a private place to relax, sloping terrain is divided into stepped terraces, entrance porch surrounded by trees

from left to right, above to below: beautiful pool with loungers, canopy and seating area make the most of the views, straight pathways divide the garden, site plan

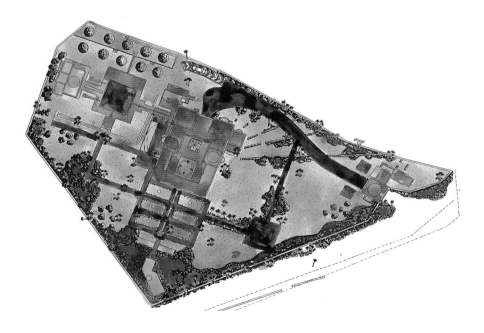

from left to right, above to below: palm trees along coast, seating
area in thatched pavilion, water cascade over pool edge

from left to right, above to below: private shaded area to lie back and relax, raised walkway with loungers and views of the ocean, seating area beneath shady tree canopy

North Island

North Island, Seychelles

Landscape architect: Patrick Watson
Architect: Silvio Rech, Lesley Carstens
Year of completion: 2003
Gross floor area: 2,000,000 m²
Design elements: guest villas, pools, beach, paved walkways
Plants: takamaka trees, badamier, coc-de-mer palm

North Island has been developed as a private resort and houses 11 villas for guests. The luxury development intends to reintroduce the Seychelles' natural flora and fauna, including giant tortoises and certain birds. The breathtaking scenery is complemented by lodge buildings, which include several renovated existing structures housing a diving center and library, as well as a number of new buildings, constructed from the removal of unwanted trees on the island. The resort is extremely private and offers a unique holiday experience, where guests can dine on the beach or follow meandering paths that wind around a landscape of waterfalls, pools, and rare tropical plants. This is the perfect place to relax, soaking up the sun and breathtaking scenery.

from left to right, above to below: site plan, water cascades over pool edge giving it a natural appearance, stepping stones, shady lounging area

from left to right, above to below: stepping stones across pool, Jacuzzi enclosed by natural-looking stone wall, palm trees along the coast

Landscape Architects'/Architects' Index

Amphibian Designs

14 Giles House 158 Westbourne
Grove
London W11 2RJ (United Kingdom)
info@amphibiandesigns.com
www.amphibiandesigns.com

AR43 Architects Pte Ltd

15a Purvis Street
Singapore 188594 (Singapore)
T +65.63334248
F +65.63334249
studio@ar43.com
www.ar43.com

Bensley Design Studios

57 Sukhumvit 61, Klongton Nua
Bangkok 10110 (Thailand)
T +66.2.3816305
bensley@bensley.co.th
www.bensley.com

nicholas burns associates

52B Nassim Hill
Singapore (Singapore)
T +65.67380064
nb@nicholas-burns.com
www.nicholas-burns.com

Camarim Arquitectos

Rua da Madalena 80
1100-322 Lisbon (Portugal)
T +351.21.8825501
mail@camarim.pt
www.camarim.pt

William Dangar + Associates

55 Cranbrook Street
Botany 2019 (Australia)
T +612.9316.9044
F +612.9316.9055
william@dangargroup.com
www.dangargroup.com

Department of Architecture Co

44 North Sathon Road
Bangkok 10500 (Thailand)
T +66.2.6339936
F +66.2.6339940
dept.of.arch@gmail.com
www.departmentofarchitecture.co.th

Philippe Dubreuil Jardiniste

20 rue de Verneuil
75007 Paris (France)
T +33.68.5303081
F +33.14.2617159
phdbubreuil@mac.com
www.philippe-dubreuil.com

DWY Landscape Architects

1543 2nd Street, Suite 101
Sarasota, FL 34236 (USA)
T +1.941.3656530
F +1.941.9554986
info@dwylandscapearchitects.com
www.DWYLandscapearchitects.com

Gil Fialho

Rua Arthur de Azevedo 636
São Paulo, 05404-001 (Brazil)
T +55.11.30624375
gilfialho@gilfialho.com.br
www.gilfialho.com.br

Francis Landscapes

2151 Building Fouad Chehab Avenue
Beirut (Lebanon)
T +961.1.502070
F +961.1.502090
findscp@inco.com.lb
www.francislandscapes.com

Guz Architects

3 Jalan Kelabu Asap
Singapore 278199 (Singapore)
T +65.64766110
F +65.74761229
guz@guzarchitects.com
www.guzarchitects.com

Alex Hanazaki Landscaping

Rua Francisco Leitão 240, casa 12
São Paulo, 05.414-020 (Brazil)
T + 55.11.30682000
contato@alexhanazaki.com.br
www.alexhanazaki.com.br.com

Hortulus Landscape Design

P.O. Box 798
Port Douglas, 4877 (Australia)
T +61.7.40991861
info@hortulus.com.au
www.hortulus.com.au

**Dennis Hundscheidt –
Palmyra Landscaping Design**

177 Young Street Sunnybank
Brisbane 4109 (Australia)
T +61.7.33456836
dhundscheidt@hotmail.com
www.dennishundscheidt.com

Joaristi & Barascout

Centro Comercial El Cruce local #20
San José (Costa Rica)
T +506.22.897660
F +506.22.898925
info@joaristibarascoutcr.com
www.joaristibarascoutcr.com

Raymond Jungles, Inc.

242 SW 5th Street
Miami, FL 33130 (USA)
T +1.305.8586777
raymond@raymondjungles.com
www.raymondjungles.com

Khosla Associates

No. 18 17th Main HAL 2nd A Stage
Bangalore 560 008 (India)
T +91.8051161445
F +91.8025294951
info@khoslaassociates.com
www.khoslaassociates.com

Leon Kluge Garden Designs

Koedoe street 9A
Nelspruit Mpumalanga, 1200
(South Africa)
T +27.82.2573525
leonkluge@yahoo.com
www.leonklugegardendesign.co.za

Leo Laniado / A Estufa

Rua Wisard, 53
São Paulo (Brazil)
T +55.11.38142300
llaniado@terra.com.br
www.aestufa.com.br

Mancini Enterprises >> 28

17 Crescent Avenue
Kesavaperumalpuram 600 028
(India)
T +91.44.24614000
architects@mancini-design.com
www.mancini-design.in

Ministry of Design >> 82

20 Cross Street #03–01
Singapore 048422 (Singapore)
T +65.62225780
studio@modonline.com
www.modonline.com

**Silvio Rech & Lesley Carstens –
Adventure Architecture** >> 218

T +27.11.4861525
adventarch@mweb.co.za

**Craig Reynolds Landscape
Architecture** >> 130, 134, 150, 158

3255 Flagler Avenue Suite 305
Key West, FL 33040 (USA)
T +1.305.2927243
www.craigreynolds.net

Exteriors by Chad Roberts >> 162, 166

2001 North 3rd Street Suite 100
Pheonix, A5 85004 (USA)
T +1.602.2526775
F +1.602.2526768
www.exteriors-cr.com

Sitetectonix Pte Ltd >> 90

51 Bras Basah Road #03-05/06
Singapore 189554 (Singapore)
T +65.63274452
F +65.63278042
helensmithyeo@sitetectonix.com
www.sitetectonix.com

Max Strang Architecture >> 146, 170

3109 Grand Avenue
Miami, FL33133 (USA)
T +1.305.3734990
F +1.305.373-4991
info@strangarchitecture.com
www.strangarchitecture.com

**VITA Planning & Landscape
Architecture** >> 154

181 3rd St, Suite 250
San Rafael, CA 94901 (USA)
T + 1.415.2590190
F + 1.415.259-0157
info@vitainc.com
www.vitainc.com

**Warner Wong Design | WOW
Architects** >> 70

30 Hill Street 01–04
Singapore 179360 (Singapore)
T +65.63333312
info@wow.sg
www.wow.sg

Patrick Watson >> 218

Isay Weinfeld >> 182, 186

Rua Wisard 305–7 Andar
São Paulo 05434-080 (Brazil)
T + 55.11.30797581
info@isayweinfeld.com
www.isayweinfeld.com

Made Wijaya >> 32, 38

Jalan Pengembak 9B Mertasari
Sanur 80228, Bali (Indonesia)
T +62.361 287668
F +62 361 286731
wlands@indosat.net.id
www.ptwijaya.com

WOHA >> 42, 86

29 Hongkong Street
Singapore 059668 (Singapore)
T +65.64234555
F +65.64234666
admin@woha.net
www.woha-architects.com

Picture Credits

Krishna Adithya	6, 8–13, 14–19
Beto Assis	190–193
Bill Bensley	6, 8–13, 14–19
Patrick Bingham-Hall	42–45, 74–77, 78–81, 82–85, 86–89
Marion Brenner Photography	174–177
Steven Brooke Photography	138–141, 142–145
CI&A Photography	70–73
David Cubero, London	110–113, 114–117, 118–121
Stephen Dunn Photography	178–181
Michelle Esposito	125 a.r.
Barry Fitzgerald	130–133, 134–137, 150–153, 158–161
Francis Landscapes, Lebanon	50–55, 223
John Gollings Photography	90–93
Demian Golovaty	206–209
Fernando Guerra, www.fernandoguerra.com	186–189
Edward Hendricks	82–85
Robin Hill	170 b.l., 172 b.l., 173
Dennis Hundscheidt	94–97
Fares Jammal	56–61, 62–65
Kym Joseph - Photography 4 Real Estate	102–105
Leon Kluge	46–49
Nelson Kon, www.nelsonkon.com.br	182–185
Albert Lim KS	66–69
David Duncan Livingston	154, 155, 156 a., 157 a. l.
Rodrigo Montoya	210–213
Mary E. Nichols	156 b.r., 157 b.r.
Nic Olshiati	198–201
Fran Parente	194–197
Bharath Ramamrutham	24–27
Prue Roscoe	106–109
Annie Schlechter Photography	126–129
Todor Spasov	166–169
John Sullivan	98–101
Wison Tungthunya	20–23
Chris van Uffelen	218–221
Claudia Uribe-Touri	146, 147, 148 b.l., 149 a.r. 170 a., b.r., 171, 172 b.r.
Greg Wilson Photography, Sarasota	122–124, 125 b., a.l.
Michael Woodall	162–165

Cover: Krishna Adithya
Backcover: from above to below, from left to right:
Stephen Dunn Photography, David Cubero (London),
Greg Wilson Photography (Sarasota)

All other pictures were made available by the architects.